I Love to Tell the Story

I Love to Tell the Story

DONNA G. ALBRECHT

BERKLEY BOOKS, NEW YORK

Permission was kindly granted to use the following:
Lyrics from "The Bible Tells Me So." Copyright © 1955 by Paramount Roy
Rogers Music Co., Inc. Copyright renewed 1983 and assigned to Paramount-Roy
Rogers Music Co., Inc.
Bil Keane cartoon copyright © 1991 by Bill Keane, Inc.

This is an original publication of The Berkley Publishing Group.

I LOVE TO TELL THE STORY

A Berkley Book / published by arrangement with
the author

PRINTING HISTORY
Berkley trade paperback edition / December 1999

The Penguin Putnam Inc. World Wide Web site address is
http://www.penguinputnam.com

ISBN: 0-425-17230-9

BERKLEY®
Berkley Books are published by The Berkley Publishing Group,
a division of Penguin Putnam Inc.,
375 Hudson Street, New York, New York 10014.
BERKLEY and the "B" design
are trademarks belonging to Penguin Putnam Inc.

PRINTED IN THE UNITED STATES OF AMERICA

10 9 8 7 6 5 4 3 2 1

Contents

NEW TESTAMENT

Acknowledgments

This book could never have been written without the gracious participation of all of the people whose stories are included here, and they have my thanks and my deepest appreciation. I would also like to thank the "gatekeepers" (personal assistants, publicists, agents, etc.) for these and the other people I approached. Their assistance in getting my interview request to the person and then frequently scheduling the interviews and handling other details is greatly appreciated.

I would like to thank the people who were there for me when I needed a special piece of information or a particular skill, including Pastor Jack and Lynne Davies, Pastor Ross Hidy, and Pastor Scott Hewes.

I would like to thank all my friends and professional colleagues who responded to my requests for suggestions on whom to approach for interviews with great names, many of whom are profiled in these pages.

With deep gratitude, I acknowledge the contribution of my literary agents, Elizabeth Pomada and Michael Larsen, in helping me find just the right publisher for this book. I would also like to thank my editor, Tom Colgan, for his support and assistance throughout this project.

I could not have done this book without the love and support of my husband, Michael, and our daughter, Abigail. They have dealt with all the challenges this book has presented with grace and humor—even when my computer crashed a week before deadline.

Most important, my thanks to God for making this book possible. I especially thank Him for helping me find the wonderful people profiled here. My dearest hope is that people who know God will get closer to Him through these pages, and people who do not know God, but who read this book because they admire the people profiled here, will get to know Him for themselves.

This book has been a joy for me to write. I hope it is a joy and a blessing for you to read.

Introduction

Bible stories have been a rich source of inspiration and a marvelous way of passing on moral lessons for countless generations. Yet, in our day-to-day lives, how often do we hear people we know or people in the public eye talk about the Bible stories that mean the most to them personally?

In our society, we often look to people who have achieved a high level of success as role models. Often, sadly, these days we are more likely to hear or read about the moral failures of some well-known people. That is considered newsworthy. Somehow the many people who strive to incorporate the moral lessons from the Bible into their daily life, and do it without a great deal of fanfare, are frequently considered less newsworthy.

In *I Love to Tell the Story*, I profile highly accomplished people who have found a strength they can count on—and the inspiration they need—to lead lives that in turn inspire others. Are they, like Mary Poppins, "practically perfect in every way?" No. They are people like any of us. Obviously they have identified their God-given talents and worked very hard to make the best possible use of them, and in their cases, that has resulted in their names being widely known.

You will notice that many of the people profiled here have had a life-altering experience that binds them to their chosen Bible story or verse, and they have been comforted, strengthened, inspired, or given the ability to deal with a difficult situation through it. You can benefit from Bible stories in the very same way both in your everyday life and when you face a crisis.

My favorite Bible story is the Story of the Talents. It is in chapter 25 of the book of St. Matthew, verses 14 through 30, and in this book is in the chapter devoted to Nichelle Nichols. In this story, a wealthy man distributes very valuable coins (called talents) to his servants before he takes a journey. While he is gone, two of his servants invest the coins; the third, too afraid of his master to risk his coin by investing it, just buries it.

When the man returns, the first two servants present him with his original investment and the profits from their ventures. The third servant simply returns the original coin, having done nothing productive with the assets with which he had been entrusted. In the story, the first two servants are honored and rewarded for their work and dedication. The other servant is banished.

One of the things I love about this story is the fact that while we still understand money and investing in much the same way as these servants, the word "talent" (with a little "t") has come to mean so much more than mere money. We each have talents that we can use to make the world a better place. I have been given some talents, including the ability to write. Your talents may be in math, music, cooking, teaching, negotiating, child care, art, athletics, writing, health care, or any number of areas.

What this story reminds me of (and frequently prods

me to deal with) is that I am expected to invest my time and energy in my talents regularly and get the most I can out of them. Are there times I don't want to? Of course! Are there times I don't always carry through the way I think I should? Unfortunately, yes. But more times than I can count, the story has helped me take the first step, then the second step, until I reached the goal that I believed I had the responsibility to achieve and had been given the talents to accomplish.

Over the years, I have often felt prodded by the story of the talents to keep trying to use all my little "t" talents the best way I can. Because of that prodding, I have built a career as a writer, done a lot of volunteer work in social service and governmental settings, and been active in my professional society. These things and the people I have gotten to know through them have enriched my life in ways I could never have imagined. All I had to do was let this Bible story give me the proverbial "kick" to get me started using my talents.

Whatever opportunities or problems you face, know that you are not alone. In fact, you are quite likely to find that one or more of the people profiled here have faced and dealt with a similar challenge themselves. When you read their stories, you may find yourself gaining new insight into ways you can improve situations that you deal with in your own life.

One of the rewarding ways of learning Bible stories has always been doing it with others. Talking with them about the ways they relate to the stories frequently opens up my mind and heart to aspects of the story that had never occurred to me. For instance, in the story of the Prodigal Son, I'd always felt that the older son who stayed home to help his father was underappreciated. Joan Wester Anderson, a firstborn like me, felt the same frustration and came to an amazing and comforting conclusion.

In this book you will read stories that make you smile, like Dale Evans's explanation of why she was standing in an airport with bananas hidden in her hat, and Lauraine Snelling's remembrances of childhood musings about whether or not Jonah could stand up inside the whale.

Other stories will amaze you with their honesty, like Michael Singletary's fight to regain truth in his life and Richard N. Bolles's decision to forgive his brother's assassin.

Since I do believe that learning how different people approach a Bible story and get something individual and unique from it helps us be open to learning new lessons and seeing new messages in stories we already thought we understood, I am delighted that a couple of stories have two people giving their viewpoints. Even if you think you know the stories of David and Goliath, and Joseph and the Many-Colored Coat, I believe you will discover something fresh and fascinating in the ways the two different people have related to each of those two stories.

Before you begin the stories, please read the next brief section that describes how I have handled the Scriptures included in this book. Thanks!

Reading the Bible Stories

Each person's story in this book begins with the Bible story or verse(s) he or she chose as a personal favorite. Their story tells how that particular Scripture has influenced—and often dramatically changed—the person's life.

I have chosen to use the King James version of the Bible for the stories in this book. I especially love the poetry and majesty of the language it uses. However, I realize that sometimes that very lovely use of language can create some confusion for readers. As a result, there will be times when you see a word or phrase in parentheses (like this). Usually that is my word or phrase, added to explain or define something.

There may be times when the spelling and punctuation of the King James version are different from the spelling and punctuation you have seen other places. I left it that way on purpose. I find that sometimes that little jolt of seeing a different spelling or way of punctuating a sentence can help me slow down my reading a bit and pay more attention.

Also, some of the stories that have been chosen by the wonderful people I interviewed were too long to include completely. In those cases, I have edited/abridged the story. I have attempted to keep the meat of the story, especially the parts that were most significant to the person I interviewed. I encourage you to read the stories in the version of the Bible you prefer (more on that in a minute).

At the beginning of each story or verse, I have given its location in the Bible and its title, such as "St. Luke 15: 11–32, The Prodigal Son." So if you want to read the story in your own Bible, go to the book of St. Luke (sometimes just called Luke), which is in the New Testament. You go to chapter 15, and the story you want to read begins with verse 11 and goes through verse 32. Where I have abridged a story, the citation gives the whole story, so you don't miss anything when you read it on your own.

I encourage you to read these stories in several different versions of the Bible as time allows. You will undoubtedly find one or more versions that speak to your heart in different ways. Some, like King James, give a sense of history and poetry in the reading. Other versions like the New Revised Standard Version, use such clear, everyday language that many people find it much easier to understand.

There are many wonderful versions of the Bible available today. A quick look through any bookstore will introduce you to Bibles that are written using different language skills, with many done in everyday language. If you are in the market for a Bible of your own, the most important thing to do is to find one that you are comfortable reading in terms of the language it contains. If you are a member of a particular faith, you might get in touch with your spiritual adviser and ask which versions of the Bible are commonly used in your religious services or study classes, because it will allow you to have continuity in your reading and studying.

There are many different features that Bible printers can offer. Two that I find particularly helpful are a concordance and a dictionary.

The concordance has words and phrases listed in alphabetical order, much like an index. Each entry has a listing of where that particular word/phrase appears in a significant way in the Bible. You can use this in several ways. First, if you have a particular subject you are interested in learning more about, you can look up words related to that subject in the concordance. Then you look up the citations listed and read what the Bible has to say on that subject.

The concordance is also an incredibly handy way to look up the origin of any Bible verse or idea that you can't quite place. For instance, in the song "Turn! Turn! Turn!" that was sung by the Byrds, there is the line "A time of love, a time of hate, a time of war, and a time of peace," that was recently going through my mind. When I look up the word "love" from that line in my Bible's concordance, here are a few listings:

LOVE (v.).
 Eccl. 3:8, a time to love
 Amos 5:15, hate the evil, and love the good
 Matt. 5:44, I say, love your enemies.

When I then go to Ecclesiastes and read chapter 3, I find the context of those words (and much of the rest of the lyrics to that song, which were adapted by Pete Seeger, who also wrote the music). So if one of those phrases (or the many others that were on the list) holds the words or idea you are looking for, you can immediately look them or it up and get the whole story.

Having a dictionary in your Bible is another handy feature. That way, when you find a word you are not familiar with, you can immediately flip back to this section and find out the meaning. The dictionary in my Bible gives a pronunciation guide and defines the terms, depending on where they occur. Since I have absolutely no personal expertise about things like the weights and measures or the clothing and military armor worn in biblical times, I find this section handy.

For instance, in the story of David and Goliath, Goliath is said to be wearing a "target between his shoulders." Well, in today's language, wearing a target between your shoulders sounds somewhat unwise, since it could be assumed that it gave the other party something to aim at. However, what they called a "target," we would call a "shield"—a much more appropriate item to wear into battle.

If you enjoy trying to envision the journeys mentioned in the Bible, you might enjoy having the maps that some Bible printers include in their volumes.

Some Bibles include writings that do not appear in many versions. Those writings are called the Apocrypha. This material is considered controversial because it is less generally accepted as authentic. While there may be exceptions, it is widely held that these writings are not considered divine revelation by biblical scholars in the Jewish and Protestant traditions, but they are in the Roman Catholic tradition.

There are all sorts of other features available in Bibles. You might prefer a Bible with notations that make it an ideal study Bible for a specific stage in life. You might like a Bible that has the words of Jesus in a different color or typeface. Some people want a Bible that contains an area for a family history and can be handed down through the generations.

However, you don't need a Bible to read this book. All of the stories and verses are right here for you. So sit back, relax, and get ready to turn the page. I want to tell you a story. . . .

Joseph and His Many-Colored Coat

Genesis 37-45

Now Israel (also known as Jacob) loved Joseph more than all his children, because he was the son of his old age: and he made him a coat of many colours. When his brethren (brothers) saw that their father loved Joseph more, they hated him.

Joseph said to his brethren, Hear, I pray you, this dream which I have dreamed: For, behold, we were binding sheaves in the field, and, lo, my sheaf arose, and also stood upright; and, behold your sheaves stood round about, and made obeisance (bowed) to my sheaf. His brethren said to him, Shalt thou indeed reign over us? They hated him yet the more for his dreams, and for his words.

Joseph dreamed yet another dream, and told it to his brethren, and said, Behold, I have dreamed a dream more; the sun and the moon and the eleven stars made obeisance to me. He told it to his father and to his brethren. His father rebuked him, and said, What is this dream that thou has dreamed? Shall I and thy mother bow down ourselves to thee? His brethren envied him; but his father observed the saying.

His brethren went to feed their father's flock. Israel said unto Joseph, I will send thee to them. Go, I pray thee, see whether it be well with thy brethren, and well with the flocks.

Joseph went after his brethren and found them in Dothan. When they saw him afar, they conspired against him to slay him. Reuben (one of the brothers) heard it, and he said unto them, Let us not kill him. Shed no blood, but cast him into this pit, that Reuben might deliver Joseph to his father again.

It came to pass when Joseph was come, they stript his coat of many colours that was on him, and cast him into a pit. They sat down to eat bread and a company of Ishmeelites came from Gilead with their camels. Judah said unto his brethren, What profit is it if we slay our brother? Come, and let us sell him to the Ishmeelites. They sold Joseph for twenty pieces of silver: and they brought Joseph into Egypt.

Reuben returned unto the pit; and, behold, Joseph was not in the pit; and he rent (ripped) his clothes. The brethren took Joseph's coat and killed a kid of the goats, and dipped the coat in the blood; they brought the coat of many colours to their father; and said, This we have found: know now whether it be thy son's coat or no. He knew it, and said, An evil beast hath devoured him. Jacob rent his clothes, and put sackcloth upon his loins, and mourned his son many days.

Joseph was brought down into Egypt; and

Potiphar, an officer of Pharaoh's, bought him. Joseph found grace in his sight, and served him: Potiphar made him overseer over his house, and all that he had he put into his hand. The Lord blessed the Egyptian's house for Joseph's sake.

It came to pass after these things, that his master's wife cast her eyes upon Joseph; and she said, Lie with me. But he refused, and said, How can I do this great wickedness, and sin against God? And it came to pass, about this time, that Joseph went into the house to do his business. She caught him by his garment, saying, Lie with me: he left his garment in her hand, and fled.

She laid up (kept) his garment by her, until his lord came home. She spake unto him, saying, The Hebrew servant came in unto me to mock me: as I lifted up my voice and cried, he left his garment with me, and fled. When his master heard the words of his wife, Joseph's master took him, and put him into the prison.

It came to pass after these things, that Pharaoh was wroth (angry) against the chief of the butlers and the chief of the bakers. He put them into the prison where Joseph was bound.

Joseph came unto them one morning, and looked upon them, and, behold, they were sad. He asked, Wherefore look ye so sadly today? They said unto him, We have dreamed a dream, and there is no interpreter of it. Joseph said unto them, Do not interpretations belong to God? tell me them, I pray you.

The chief butler told his dream. Joseph said

unto him, This is the interpretation of it: Within three days shall Pharaoh lift up thine head, and restore thee unto thy place: after the former manner when thou wast his butler. But think on me when it shall be well with thee. When the chief baker saw that the interpretation was good, he said his dream to Joseph. Joseph answered and said, This is the interpretation thereof: Within three days shall Pharaoh lift up thy head from thee, and shall hang thee on a tree. And it came to pass.

At the end of two full years, Pharaoh dreamed: and, behold, he stood by the river. There came up out of the river seven well favoured kine (cattle) and fatfleshed. Behold, seven other kine came up after them, ill favored and leanfleshed. The ill favored did eat up the seven well favored. So Pharaoh awoke. Then he slept and dreamed the second time: behold, seven good ears of corn came up upon one stalk. Then seven thin ears sprung up after them and the thin ears devoured the good ears.

It came to pass in the morning that his spirit was troubled; and he called for all the magicians of Egypt, and all the wise men thereof: and Pharaoh told them his dream; but there was none that could interpret them.

Then spake the chief butler unto Pharaoh, saying, I do remember. There was (in prison) a young man, an Hebrew. He interpreted (our dreams) to us, so it was; me he restored unto mine office, and him he hanged.

Pharaoh sent and called Joseph and they brought him hastily out of the dungeon. Pharaoh said unto Joseph, I have dreamed a dream, and there is none that interpret it: I have heard say of thee, that thou canst understand a dream to interpret it. Joseph answered, saying, It is not in me: God shall give Pharaoh an answer of peace. Then Pharaoh told Joseph his dreams.

Joseph said unto Pharaoh, The dream of Pharaoh is one: God has shewed Pharaoh what he is about to do. The seven good kine are seven years; and the seven good ears are seven years: the dream is one. The seven thin kine and empty ears shall be seven years of famine. Behold, there come seven years of great plenty throughout all the land of Egypt: and there shall arise after them seven years of famine. Now therefore let Pharaoh look out a man discreet and wise, and set him over the land. Let him appoint officers, and take up the fifth part of the land in the seven plenteous years. That food shall be for store against the seven years of famine.

Pharaoh said unto Joseph, Forasmuch as God hath shewed thee all this: thou shalt be over my house, and according unto thy word shall all my people be ruled: only in the throne will I be greater than thou.

Now when Jacob saw that there was corn in Egypt, he said unto his sons, Get you down thither, and buy for us; that we may live. Joseph's ten brethren went to buy corn in Egypt. Joseph was the governor over the land, and he it was that sold to all the people of the land: his brethren came, and bowed down before him. Joseph saw his brethren and knew them, but they knew him not. And he remembered the dreams which he dreamed of them.

And Joseph said unto his brethren, I am Joseph, your brother, whom ye sold into Egypt. Now therefore, be not grieved, nor angry with yourselves, that ye sold me hither: for God did send me before you to preserve life. So now it was not you that sent me hither, but God.

Mark Victor Hansen

Mark Victor Hansen is a highly sought-after motivational speaker and best-selling author. His credits include Future Diary *and* How to Achieve Total Prosperity, *and he is coauthor of the books of the wildly successful* Chicken Soup *series.*

"I think the most important line in the Bible happens to be in the story of Joseph and His Many-Colored Coat, where you had a man go from a pauper to a prisoner to leading a whole country," says Mark. "The line I think is so critical is 'What you meant for my harm'—when his brothers put him away—'God meant for my good.' "

Like Joseph, Mark knows what it is to go through hard times. There was a period in the 1960s where his life seemed as charmed as that of Joseph. While Joseph was the favorite son and golden boy of his family, Mark was a shining success in business. After meeting Buckminster Fuller while in graduate school at Southern Illinois University (Mark later completed his Ph.D. at Golden State University), Mark threw his lot in with Fuller, who created geodesic dome homes and was soon selling millior dollars' worth of them every year. A primary element in those homes was made of petroleum products (PVC).

Then the Arab oil embargo hit.

"When I was going upside down and wanted to kill myself, I began to understand this line of Joseph's," Mark states thoughtfully. "What I thought the oil embargo meant for my harm, God meant for my good, because what it did was get me out of what I shouldn't be doing—which was selling tangibles and building geodesic domes—and into what I should be doing, which is speaking, writing, communicating, marketing, and promoting. What I am today is a merchant of hope and an information utility."

But moving from selling domes to becoming a speaker and writer was no more a smooth transition for him than going from being a shepherd to being second in command to Pharaoh was for Joseph.

First, there was the matter of the bankruptcy. For a man who had been flying high, dealing with his bankruptcy brought Mark so low that he contemplated suicide more than once. When he thought of going to his brothers for financial help, all he could imagine was their saying, "Look, you just went bankrupt for $2 million! You tried to borrow money from us. You tried to do all these cockamamie things. Why don't you go get a job?" To him, this was the equivalent of Joseph's being thrown in the well by his brothers.

When he heard the story of Joseph during this life-changing time, Mark says he finally "got it." "I probably heard it in church when I was a little kid and didn't get it. But all of a sudden you get hit in the face a couple of times, what I like to say is 'get thunked.' Everybody gets thunked—with a health issue, a financial issue, a relationship issue. We've all got our own issues. But the point is, when you get thunked, it can either evaporate you or re-create you. What Cavett Robert, my great motivational teacher and Dean of Professional Speakers, used to say is 'Life is a grindstone. It either grinds you down or polishes you up.' "

Mark continues by explaining that everyone goes through times where they feel they are being harmed, or metaphorically thrown in the well, by other people. Often by people who are very close to them. He adds that everyone is going to have seven years, seven days, seven minutes, or seven seconds of suffering. "Everybody's got these stories, and what you've got to know is that if you can hang in long enough, you're going to get through your story. It doesn't matter who doesn't support you, because what they meant for your harm, God meant for your good. I think it ought to be highlighted and in bold print in the Bible!"

Along with understanding that God can help bring good results from bad times, Mark notes that forgiveness is an important element in these kinds of situations. "The people closest to you don't necessarily mean to betray you," he explains. "That's why forgiveness is such a major issue in the world. You've got to be forgiving.

"So going bankrupt was my best/worst experience," Mark continues. "It got me out. When I wanted to kill myself thirty years ago, I said, 'What is it I really want to do?' And I said, 'The real reason I was following Bucky is I wanted to speak. I wanted to talk to people and change their lives, motivate them, and move them to fulfill their respective destinies.' "

So Mark turned his focus from the life that was in shambles to creating the life he really wanted to live. Not that everything immediately fell into place. Among the challenges was the work of selling the first *Chicken Soup* book to a publisher. Thirty-three publishers rejected it before he and Jack Canfield found Health Communications, Inc. But even after HCI offered to publish it, they did not have terribly high hopes. They thought it might—might—sell 20,000 copies before going out of print. That was 25 million book sales ago.

Remembering that it was Pharaoh who gave Joseph a chance to use his God-given gifts to their fullest, Mark describes his publisher as being his Pharaoh because they recognized that he had a tremendous dream and they made it possible for him to achieve it.

"Everybody has a dream," Mark states. He notes that the Bible says that without vision, or a dream in our heart, people perish. Looking at it from another angle, he suggests that with vision, people will flourish. If, unlike Joseph, people cannot interpret their own dreams, Mark tells them to find someone they are close to—and trust—to help them interpret their dreams and discover their soul's mission.

"Like Joseph, I'm on my soul's mission," Mark says emphatically. "I'm supposed to be a storyteller and provocateur. The story of Joseph and His Many-Colored Coat works for me. At every level, it works for me."

Michael Chang

At seventeen, Michael became the youngest player ever to win a tennis Grand Slam event when he won the 1989 French Open. In the years since then, his hard work has enabled him to have many high-ranking years (he was ranked #2 for parts of both 1996 and 1997). Michael also works hard off the court to help children achieve their goals through his Tennis Stars of the Future program in Hong Kong, being involved with the ATP charity events, and by setting up the Chang Family Tennis Scholarship Fund at the University of California, Berkeley. He, too, selected the story of Joseph and His Coat of Many Colors.

"I think that with all the stories, each time you go back, it seems as if God shows you something new, and that's one of the wonders about reading God's word," says Michael. His words are not only true of one person reading the same story over again; they are clearly shown in the ways that two people can understand the basic message in the same story in different ways. In this story, Mark Victor Hansen saw a victory for forgiveness. Reading the same Bible story, Michael finds a message of persevering and overcoming the odds.

"I think Joseph had a lot of trials that he went through," says Michael. "He had times where he was following the Lord, but yet, he had to go through hard times. I think in many aspects, his faith was really tested even when he did things that were right in the eyes of the Lord. Just things like with Potiphar's wife having him imprisoned when her seduction attempt failed, and the butler forgetting about him after he helped him get out of prison. Yet through all of it, he was still faithful. In the end, God really blessed him and used the time that was difficult for him in a blessing that he didn't see until later.

"I think that in certain ways, for me, particularly in the past year, things have been tough. I've gone through a couple of major injuries this year." Michael took a bad fall on a wet and slippery court when he was practicing to defend one of his titles. The result was a painful tear of one of the ligaments in his left knee. For seven weeks, Michael was unable to compete. Then the wrist he had been overtaxing to compensate for the knee injury developed tendinitis. This injury proved to be the more devastating because it continued for over seven months, and forced him to miss tournaments and default matches. As a result, his ranking went from #3 at the end of the 1997 season to a disappointing #29 at the end of 1998. Of the last year, Michael says, "I've only been able to play about a handful of tournaments injury-free, and that has really contributed to the ranking fall."

Even as he had praised and thanked God publicly when he won the 1989 French Open, Michael continued to be faithful when things were not going well. He found that at difficult times, it is good to rediscover the story of Joseph and his faithfulness.

"God definitely had great plans in store for him [Joseph]. I would think that under normal circumstances, for anybody to go through something like that and be misunderstood, to be hated by your brothers, and having to go through all of those things, it is pretty amazing that he was still so faithful and at the same time was able to go and serve the Lord in a way that was a great example." Michael adds with emphasis, "Think about when he was in prison: to be just a model person there; to be put in charge of so many different things; his attitude was pretty amazing!"

When asked if thinking of Joseph was a personal help during this difficult year, Michael answered unequivocally: "Absolutely! I've learned a lot of things this year. Sometimes it takes a tough situation or going through tough times in order for you to stop and be able to realize what God is trying to say. The last couple of years, I've gotten so close to becoming #1. During the off-season last year, I worked really, really hard, thinking that if I put a little bit of extra effort into it, I'd be able to get to that #1 spot. I'd be able to break through and win the next Grand Slam tournaments. God showed me something totally different, and really opened my eyes to know and realize that things don't happen because of my strength, but because of His. That the talent I have, the talent that He has given me, is not a talent that I've earned in any respect.

"I definitely am learning to trust Him and stay positive, and also not to lose hope. I think in today's society it's too easy to give up and to quit—to take the easy way out. I feel like in my life, God has wanted me to persevere and to stay hopeful and constantly trust in Him, because through a difficult time, God can use that to really touch people's lives. Not just to give me hope, but to give other people hope as well."

Along with learning more about trust, Michael finds that his recent experiences have given him a new appreciation for what he has. "I've had a pretty much injury-free career [except for a hip fracture at the end of 1989], so injuries were never something that I thought too much about," Michael says. He mentions that one thing that has been impressed on him during the 1998 season is "You definitely learn to be thankful for the good times and also thankful through the difficult times, because you know that through the difficult times, God matures you—grows you in character. I think in many instances, God prepares you for bigger and better things that He wants you to be a part of."

Acknowledging that his problems have been difficult for him, he calls them "peanuts" compared to the problems that many other people face every day. "I think that for every individual who lives here on Earth, there are going to be good times and bad times. I think everybody can handle the good times, but the bad times are where people are tested and their faith is tested. There are so many stories in the Bible, and I think Joseph is a great example of going through tough times, not losing that hope, not losing that trust in God."

Michael continues, "Sometimes I almost feel like people quit just before God is able to really take that situation and make something good out of it. You have to give God that opportunity. It's not easy going through difficult times, by any means, but the comfort is that God understands, and through it all, God has a perfect purpose. I believe that He uses everything for good."

Moses Wants to See God's Glory

Exodus 33:18-23

He (Moses) said, I beseech thee, shew me thy glory. God said, I will make all my goodness pass before thee, and I will proclaim the name of the Lord before thee; and will be gracious to whom I will be gracious, and will shew mercy on whom I will shew mercy. He said, Thou canst not see my face: for there shall no man see me, and live. The Lord said, Behold, there is a place by me, and thou shalt stand upon a rock: it shall come to pass, while my glory passeth by, that I will put thee in a clift (cleft) of the rock, and will cover thee with my hand while I pass by: I will take away mine hand, and thou shalt see my back parts: but my face shall not be seen.

Michael Medved

Known to millions of listeners of over a hundred radio stations throughout the country for his topical and compelling Michael Medved Show, *Michael is also the author of eight books, including* Saving Childhood: Protecting Our Children from the National Assault on Innocence. *His interests range from the quirky Golden Turkey Awards he originated in his work as a movie critic, to the significant work he has done as cofounder of the Pacific Jewish Center in California. Of his life, Michael says, "I'm trying to make difficult and imperfect—but well-meaning—efforts to combine a media career with an observant Jewish life."*

"I think that this is the most revealing story, because what it suggests, of course, is that while we are living life in the moment, it is difficult to discern the divine role, the divine presence." Michael explains, "It is much easier, and indeed more possible, to view that divine presence in retrospect. We can see God's back, but never His face. Again, it applies to historic events. It applies to personal events.

"There are tons of examples," Michael says. "One example might be looking at the 1967 war in Israel. That clearly was a terrible time. It was a time when people who lived in Israel—about three million people—felt that their lives were in grave danger. It was very hard and humbling to think that that Gamal Abdel Nasser and other Arab leaders who were fomenting that war could be some kind of divine hand or divine plan.

"Afterward, with the Jewish people in control of (the eastern half) of Jerusalem again, really for the first time in two thousand years, it was very hard *not* to see the hand of God in some of those events. The idea that it was six days and on the seventh day they rested, all of that, to many people is a clear indication of God's role."

Michael mentions another example from recent history where the hand of God is unseen during the crisis but becomes obvious when people have come through the event and can look back on it. This example was brought to him by his father, who was living in Israel at the time. "During the Gulf War in 1991, the people were terrified of Scud missile attacks and absolutely horrified about what was going on. Israel was not at war with Iraq. It had taken no aggressive action against Iraq. Yet Israel was being hit with these missiles. The amazing thing, that became clear afterward, is that no one died. Thirty-nine missiles struck the soil of Israel! Many people pointed out, including secular people, that the number is associated with the number of lashes you could get in biblical times as punishment for something. So it was seen that it was thirty-nine. It wasn't thirty-seven. It wasn't forty-one. It was thirty-nine Scud missiles that had landed in Israel. And yet, though there was a great deal of destruction and punishment, there was no death penalty. No one had died, and that seemed to be a significant indication of God's plan."

Michael adds that all of the evidence of God's hand in human life does not appear on such a large scale. Often, God works in the lives of individuals in ways that also are evident only in retrospect.

Michael tells of a friend who had a marvelous detour that seemed like a major headache at the time. "A friend of mine was trying to get home for the very important holiday of Shavuot (known to Christians as Pentecost). This is one of those holidays where if you're observant and Jewish, you don't travel. You don't travel in airplanes. You don't travel in cars.

"In any event, she had to switch planes in Pittsburgh and, horrifyingly, the flight was canceled. She was stuck in a city she'd never been in before. It was cold. It was miserable. She didn't know anybody and desperately made a few calls to try to see if she could connect with the Jewish community in Pittsburgh because she couldn't make it home to California. In any event, she met her husband over that weekend and now lives in Pittsburgh with their children."

Michael concludes his explanation about why this story from Exodus is so important to him: "This can be applied time and time again, which is precisely why I would say it's my favorite biblical story. Even Moses, who after all, knows more about God—is God's dictation agent in terms of passing on key information (including the Ten Commandments)—even Moses is shown that his knowledge of God is going to come from watching God's back from (behind) a rock."

So Michael encourages people to think back on challenging times in their lives and consider how God helped them through those times, and perhaps used those events to help in unexpected ways. Maybe when you look back, you will realize you were part of a crisis that changed the world, like the Israeli people regaining the holy city of Jerusalem in the 1967 war. Maybe another challenge you faced changed your life, like Michael's friend who found love and a husband because of a canceled airline flight. Like Moses, when you look and see the back of God's glory, it can give you a fresh appreciation of the ways you are being taken care of, especially during the difficult times.

The Story
of Gideon

Judges 6:11-8:3

There came an angel of the Lord, and sat under an oak which was in Ophrah, that pertained unto (was owned by) Joash, the Abiezrite: and his son Gideon threshed wheat by the wine-press, to hide it from the Midianites.

The angel of the Lord appeared unto him, and said unto him, The Lord is with thee, thou mighty man of valour. And Gideon said unto him, Oh my Lord, if the Lord be with us, why is all this befallen us?

The Lord looked upon him, and said, Go in this thy might, and thou shalt save Israel from the hand of the Midianites: have not I sent thee? Gideon said unto him, Oh my Lord, wherewith shall I save Israel? behold, my family is poor in Manasseh, and I am the least in my father's house. The Lord said to him, Surely I will be with thee, and thou shalt smite (kill) the Midianites as one man.

It came to pass the same night, that the Lord said unto Gideon, Take thy father's young bullock, even the second bullock of seven years old, and throw down the altar of Baal (an idol) that thy father hath, and cut down the grove that is by it: build an altar unto the Lord thy God upon the top of this rock, and take the second bullock, and offer a burnt sacrifice with the wood of the grove which thou shalt cut down. Then Gideon took ten men of his servants, and did as the Lord had said unto him.

When the men of the city arose early in the morning, behold, the altar of Baal was cast down, the grove was cut down that was by it, and the second bullock was offered upon the altar that was built. They said to one another, Who hath done this thing? When they asked, they said, Gideon, the son of Joash hath done this thing. Then the men of the city said unto Joash, Bring out thy son, that he may die: because he hath cast down the altar of Baal. Joash said, Will ye plead for Baal? if he be a god, let him plead for himself.

(Later) The Spirit of the Lord came upon Gideon, and he blew a trumpet; and (the people of) Abiezer gathered after him.

Then Gideon, and all the people that were with him, rose up early, and pitched beside the well of Harod: so that the host of the Midianites were on the north side of them. The Lord said unto Gideon, The people that are with thee are too many for me to give the Midianites into their hands, lest Israel vaunt themselves against me saying, Mine own hand hath saved me. Now therefore go to, proclaim in the ears of the people saying, Whosoever is fearful and afraid, let him return and depart early. And there returned of the people twenty and two thousand; and there remained ten thousand.

Then the Lord said to Gideon, The people are yet too many; bring them down unto the water. Every one that lappeth of the water with his tongue, as a dog lappeth, him shalt thou set by himself; likewise every one that boweth down upon his knees to drink. The number of them that lapped, putting their hand to their mouth, were three hundred men. And the Lord said unto Gideon, By the three hundred men that lapped will I save you, and deliver the Midianites into thine hand.

It came to pass the same night, that the Lord said unto him, Arise, get thee down unto the host (army); for I have delivered it into thine hand. But if thou fear to go down, go thou with Phurah thy servant down to the host and thou shalt hear what they say; afterward shall thine hands be strengthened.

When Gideon was come (gone down to spy on the Midianites), behold, there was a man that told a dream unto his fellow, and said, Behold, I dreamed a dream, and, lo, a cake of barley bread tumbled into the host of Midian and smote it. And his fellow answered and said, This is nothing else save the sword of Gideon the son of Joash, a man of Israel: for into his hand hath God delivered Midian, and all the host.

When Gideon heard the telling of the dream, and the interpretation thereof, he worshipped and returned into the host of Israel, and said, Arise; for the Lord hath delivered into your hand the host of Midian. He divided the three hundred men into three companies, and he put a trumpet in every man's hand, with empty pitchers, and lamps within the pitchers.

And he said unto them, Look on me, and do likewise: when I blow with a trumpet, I and all that are with me, then blow ye the trumpets also on every side of the camp, and say, The sword of the Lord, and of Gideon. So Gideon, and the men that were with him, came unto the outside of the camp: and they blew the trumpets, and brake the pitchers that were in their hands (so the torches would show). The three hundred blew the trumpets, and the Lord set every man's sword against his fellow, even throughout all the host: and the host fled. The men of Israel gathered themselves together and pursued after the Midianites. They took two princes of the Midianites, Oreb and Zeeb; and they slew them and brought their heads to Gideon.

The men of Ephraim said unto Gideon, Why has thou served us thus, that thou calledst us not, when thou wentest to fight with the Midianites? And they did chide with him sharply. Gideon said unto them, What have I done now in comparison of you? God hath delivered into your hands the princes of Midian, Oreb and Zeeb; and what was I able to do in comparison of you? Then their anger was abated toward him, when he had said that.

Zig Ziglar

A world-renowned motivational speaker, Zig Ziglar is also the author of several best-selling books, including See You at the Top *and* Over the Top.

"I identify with Gideon's reluctance to get involved in the fray," Zig Ziglar says thoughtfully. "I think most of us, when God gives us big marching orders, are inclined to say, 'Lord, give me a little deal. I can handle it.

"I think most of us are that way. God let me wander around for forty-five years, relying entirely on my own skills and talents, personality and ability. I was an honest, hardworking, motivated guy. But until Christ entered my life and I tapped into His power, I was struggling, and my career was going nowhere. When I started to heed the biblical principles, things really started to happen, because I realized that I didn't have to do it all. I had all kinds of help, and that made it lots easier."

Since he became a Christian, Ziglar has seen the story of Gideon from a fresh perspective. Once, it was a stirring tale of battles and conquest. Now it is so much more. Every time he reads the story, he finds layers and layers of lessons that help him recognize how God works in his life by understanding the ways God worked in Gideon's life.

Ziglar recounts, "I would say, first of all, that God took a nation that was incomplete; awash in abject negativism, disarray, and reduced to bare minimums. Then the angel of the Lord appeared before Gideon. He gave Gideon a rather interesting salutation when he said to him, in essence, 'You mighty soldier of the lord.' That stunned Gideon, who responded, in the modern-day vernacular, 'Who, me? Why, my family is the least of all, and I am the runt of the litter. Why on earth would you call me a mighty warrior?' " At that time, Gideon was hiding by a winepress, threshing wheat, where he would not be found by the conquering Midianites. Hardly a warrior-like act. Yet, the angel commissioned him to deliver Israel from its enemies.

Ziglar states, "God chose the lowest family of the nation and selected the runt of that litter. Then he sent his Holy Spirit to be with Gideon, and as the old saying goes, 'You plus God equals enough!' That's my favorite part of the story of Gideon.

"Another thing I like about it is that it comes in increments," Ziglar continues. "The Lord manifests Himself and says, 'Just to let you know I'm in on this deal, I'm going to give you a plan of action. Here's step 1. Let's shake up the confidence of the people in Baal and restore it to me. We're going to get rid of Baal in no uncertain terms, and that's not going to be a problem for you." And it wasn't!

Next Gideon raises an army of thirty-two thousand people and God tells him how to winnow it down in stages until he has three hundred warriors. "Well, I'm certain that Gideon, by now, is skeptical," Ziglar says with a chuckle. "Gideon thought, 'Lord, I have three hundred and they've got over a hundred thousand or so out there!' God knew Gideon was a little nervous, and said, 'Why don't you go down there and listen in on what those dudes are saying?'

"Of course, when he went down and listened, one of them was telling about this troubling dream. Then his friend said, 'Oh, that means that Gideon can come in and do away with us!' When Gideon heard this, he praised God and went back to gather his troops for battle.

"I like the next part of it too," Ziglar adds. "Because even though Gideon was under the influence of the Holy Spirit, he still was recognizing the fact that he was the leader and they needed a battle plan. As humans we are supposed to use the judgment, wisdom, and common sense our Lord has given us.

"What Gideon did was divide his troops into three camps and take up the pitchers and trumpets that had been discarded by the soldiers who left earlier. So all three hundred of Gideon's men were armed with lamps, pitchers (to put over the lamps to hide the light from the enemies), and trumpets. At Gideon's signal they blew the trumpets on all sides, broke their pitchers so their torches blazed, and they shouted for the Lord and Gideon. Instantly, turmoil broke out and the enemy probably thought there were hundreds of thousands of them. In their panic they started killing each other. You know," Ziglar continues thoughtfully, "that, to me, was rather fascinating, because it shows that the Lord not only aids us, but He disturbs the enemy, breeding panic and confusion among them. He used Gideon to do it. He didn't need anybody, of course, but He used Gideon and his trumpets and lamps for His purpose. When panic broke out, the Midianites, in their confusion, started killing each other. Gideon's people were in mass pursuit and they killed over 120,000 of the enemy."

With enthusiasm Ziglar adds, "I like the fact that they weren't content to just rout the enemy at that point, but he realized that they had to destroy them or they wouldn't have any security. So Gideon followed through—and good follow-through is important. These are some of the lessons I like out of the story of Gideon.

"Here's the interesting thing," Ziglar continues conspiratorially. "Even after all that, the tribal leaders of Israel were violently angry with Gideon, wanting to know why he didn't let them in on his plans from the beginning. You know, pride and jealousy are interesting, very destructive forces. Pride, in this instance, is not genuine pride, but false pride or vanity.

"I like this part because I'm a salesman and always will be. Gideon gave a very diplomatic sales response to these egotists when he said, 'God let you capture Oreb and Zeeb, and the generals of the army admit that what I did is nothing compared to what you did.' Gideon clearly understood that God had won the victory."

When you listen to Ziglar, the story of Gideon comes alive on so many levels. As he sees it, Gideon helps everyone realize that even if they consider themselves to be no one special, if they trust God, they can accomplish more than they ever dreamt. "Well, I know where I was when God took over," Ziglar concludes, "and I know where I am now. There's a substantial difference!"

Saul's Inappropriate Sacrifices

1 Samuel 13:1-14

Saul reigned one year; and when he had reigned two years over Israel, Saul chose him three thousand men of Israel; whereof two thousand were with Saul in Michmash and in mount Bethel, and a thousand were with Jonathan in Gibeah of Benjamin: and the rest of the people he sent every man to his tent. Jonathan smote (defeated) the garrison of the Philistines that was in Geba, and the Philistines heard of it. Saul blew the trumpet throughout all the land, saying, Let the Hebrews hear. All Israel heard that Saul had smitten a garrison of the Philistines, and that Israel also was had in abomination with the Philistines (Israel was intensely disliked by the Philistines). The people were called together after Saul to Gilgal.

The Philistines gathered themselves together to fight with Israel, thirty thousand chariots, and six thousand horsemen, and people as the sand which is on the sea shore in multitude: and they came up, and pitched in Michmash, eastward from Bethaven. When the men of Israel saw that they were in a strait (for the people were distressed), then the people did hide themselves in caves, and in thickets, and in rocks, and in high places, and in pits. Some of the Hebrews went over Jordan to the land of Gad and Gilead. As for Saul, he was yet in Gilgal, and all the people followed him trembling.

He tarried (waited) seven days, according to the set time that Samuel had appointed: but Samuel came not to Gilgal; and the people were scattered from him. Saul said, Bring hither a burnt offering to me, and peace offerings. He offered the burnt offering. It came to pass, that as soon as he had made an end of offering the burnt offering, behold, Samuel came; and Saul went out to meet him, that he might salute him.

Samuel said, What has thou done? Saul said, Because I saw the people were scattered from me, and that thou camest not within the days appointed, and that the Philistines gathered themselves together at Michmash; Therefore said I, The Philistines will come down now upon me to Gilgal, and I have not made supplication unto the Lord: I forced myself therefore, and offered a burnt offering. Samuel said to Saul, Thou hast done foolishly: thou hast not kept the commandment of the Lord thy God, which he commanded thee: for now would the Lord have established thy kingdom upon Israel for ever. But now thy kingdom shall not continue: the Lord hath sought him a man after his own heart, and the Lord hath commanded him to be captain over his people, because thou hast not kept that which the Lord commanded thee.

Gloria Gaynor

❦

World-renowned singer Gloria Gaynor was crowned "Queen of Disco" in 1976 because of her distinctive musical performances, including her international hit record, I Will Survive. *She continues to sing and tour internationally, as well as record new albums. Her latest,* It's My Time, *was released first in Europe in January 1999. It was shipped "gold" (best-seller) and should be available in U.S. record stores soon. Gloria balances the demands of her career with an active volunteer schedule that includes being on the board of the Bergen County United Cerebral Palsy Assn., working for several other charitable organizations, and being the official godmother for the French World Cup Champion soccer team. She notes proudly that this is quite an honor. Team jerseys numbered 1–22 are worn by team members, #23 is worn by the president of France, and #24 is hers.*

At first glance, this Bible story might seem to be a somewhat unusual choice, but to Gloria, it is just perfect. She explains, "I've found myself referring to it over the years a number of times. It reminds me to make sure the decisions I make about my career, about my life, are of God and not just my ego. That it is God's will. Because I know that if that's not what happens, you miss out on God's blessings."

Gloria was raised with a rudimentary faith, but for many years it was not the center of her life. In her autobiography, *I Will Survive* (St. Martin's Press, 1997), she recalls, "She [my mother] read the Bible. But it seemed to me that she read the Bible as if it were a novel. But the real reason why I didn't do wrong as a child was that I loved my mother. I never wanted to hurt her." That's not to say she didn't believe in God. She notes that until the day her mother died, the extent of Gloria's relationship with God was that "I would give Him my nightly grocery list, and in exchange I tried to be a good and moral person. That was the deal. There was nothing more to it than that. After she passed away in 1970, I became more aware of a great emptiness in the center of my life."

While her mother had been a very positive and loving influence in Gloria's life, there were other, less positive, things happening. "I was raised without a father, and I think that has a great influence on a girl's life. A negative influence. I think that that had caused me from time to time to make wrong decisions. But after having become a Christian, I've learned to trust God as my father and I've benefited very much."

One instance that readily comes to her mind and relates directly to her Bible story involved what Gloria calls a "cash flow shortage." During this time, many years ago, she had run up bills on two credit cards. One was for $578 and the other one was for over $5,000. Since being a singer does not provide a regular income like some jobs, there can be times when it is hard to pay the bills.

During one particularly challenging time, Gloria's lawyer reviewed her financial situation and advised her that she should consider filing for bankruptcy. She recalls, "He said that when you file for bankruptcy, you stop paying your bills and you include that stuff in your bankruptcy. So I had stopped paying my bills. I found out after a while that that wasn't the best thing to do, because if I wasn't planning on being broke for the next seven years, whatever money I did make within that time would be wiped out by the old debts anyway, and I wouldn't be able to get any credit. I wouldn't be able to do anything. I thought, 'Oh man, I don't think this is the optimum thing to do.' "

On discovering the long-term problems associated with declaring bankruptcy, Gloria decided not to. However, by this time she had not been paying on those two credit cards for quite a while.

Soon she received a call from the credit card company with the $578 balance, demanding payment. "He called me on a Thursday and I asked him to call me back on Monday and I would tell him how I would deal with it," Gloria says. "So over the weekend I fasted and prayed and the Lord told me to tell the man that I would pay $50 a month until the bill was paid. So on Monday, I told him I'd pay $50 a month and he said, 'You'll have to send me a check for $78 and then send me ten postdated checks for $50 each.' "

"So I sent him the checks and I told my husband about it and he was like, 'How can you do that? What makes you think you're going to have that $50 per month? We don't know what's going to happen. We don't know what's coming in.' And I said, 'Well, look, I really believe that God told me to do that, and so I've done it.' And for those months, this $50 was coming in and I was able to pay it. I was able to make sure the money was in the bank to cover the checks, and everything was going along fine.

"Then I got a call for the $5,000 bill. So I told him, 'Well, can you call me back tomorrow?' So he called back the next day, and I told him that I would pay $500 per month until this bill was paid, and he said, 'OK, now you have to send me the ten postdated checks and another check for the overage immediately.' I said 'OK,' and told my husband what I was going to do. He was raving! I said, 'Don't worry about it. God's going to take care of it.' Then I called a friend to ask her for the first $500, and she told me that she would send the money that weekend."

But even though the two situations seemed nearly identical at first glance, Gloria had omitted the most important step in trying to figure out what she should do. The first time the problem arose, she prayed for guidance. The second time, she assumed she knew the answer.

In the first situation, the money started rolling in from expected and unexpected sources. Not huge amounts, but enough to allow her to pay the bills. This second time, things started out badly when her friend never delivered the promised $500 for the first payment.

After days of calling everyone she could think of, Gloria was growing frantic. The first of the checks she had sent the credit card company was due to hit the bank any day, and there still wasn't any money there to cover it. Gloria remembers crying out to the Lord, " 'Why hasn't this girl called me back? Why hasn't this money come in? I trusted you! I don't understand—you said you would supply all of my needs according to your riches.' And the Lord said to me, 'But I didn't say I was going to give you this money.

The first time, you took the time and you asked me and I told you how to deal with it. I told you that I would supply your needs. But this time, you didn't ask me. You assumed that I would deal with it the way you thought it should be dealt with.' I thought, 'I'm sorry, Lord,' and He answered, 'Don't take me for granted.' "

Gloria adds, "The Lord deals with me in parables, and I just really love it. He said to me, 'If you were out in the street and you saw your friends had skates and came in and asked your mother for skates, she might tell you to go get her credit card, go to the store, and get yourself a pair of skates. OK, you get your skates, you're happy. Everything is great. Now, the next time, you see your friends with bikes and you want a bike. You go in the house and get your mother's credit card and you go and get yourself a bike. How do you think she's going to feel about that? Maybe she would have bought you the bike. Maybe she would have told you to go and get her credit card and get yourself a bike. But you don't just go and get her credit card and get yourself a bike. So this is what you have done with me.'

"Well, I was on my knees crying and repenting, and He says, 'OK, just dry up and learn this lesson. Understand that you do not take me for granted, because you don't know how I might decide to take care of your problem. Now call your friend Carol.' "

Well, Gloria still hadn't completely decided to trust and obey. She thought that Carol might not have the money right away, so she called others first—and was turned down, of course. When she finally gave up and called Carol, she heard, "Oh, if you had called me fifteen minutes ago, I could have given it to you in cash. I just put it in the bank."

Well, in the end, Carol did come through, as God had told Gloria she would. When she recounted this experience to another friend, Gloria was told that her attempts to control the situation sounded like they had too many "*o*'s" in them. When asked what that meant, the friend explained, "It's good, but it's not God."

Gloria says that like Saul's decision to make the sacrifice at the wrong time, she has been headstrong in some of the ways she has tried to deal with her problems.

At the end of the Bible story, Saul has forfeited the chance to rule all Israel because of his headstrong attitude. Gloria notes that this one act was not an isolated incident that caused God to punish Saul. "This is the wisdom that has come to me in learning the Word and learning the ways of God: It wasn't one thing. That one thing just showed Saul himself his own character. It sort of allowed God to say, 'See, this is who you really are, and this is why I can't allow you to be over the kingdom.' "

When asked if she believes everyone should fear that they are only one mistake away from losing out on the best things that can happen in their lives, Gloria says absolutely not. "I've never felt that. I think the only way that happens is if you are willful and you're saying to God, 'This is the way I want to do it. I don't care what you want.' I think you even have to try His patience, because God has so much patience.

"So when I think of this story, it reminds me that I really need to think, search in my heart, and search in the Scriptures. I just sit in prayer and listen for God's guidance and instruction, so as to not make the wrong decisions. To know that if I really believe in my heart that I've received instructions, I can trust that He knows what He's doing, even when I don't."

David and Goliath

1 Samuel 17

Now the Philistines gathered together their armies to battle, and were gathered together at Shochoh. The Philistines stood on a mountain on the one side, and Israel stood on a mountain on the other side: and there was a valley between them.

There went out a champion out of the camp of the Philistines, named Goliath, of Gath, whose height was six cubits and a span (nine feet, nine inches). He had an helmet of brass upon his head, and he was armed with a coat of mail; and the weight of the coat was five thousand shekels of brass (about 150 pounds). He had greaves of brass (armor covering from ankle to knee) upon his legs, and a target (shield) of brass between his shoulders. The staff of his spear was like a weaver's beam; and his spear's head weighed six hundred shekels (about twenty pounds) of iron: and one bearing a shield went before him. He stood and cried unto the armies of Israel, and said unto them, Why are ye come out to set your battle in array? am not I a Philistine and ye servants to Saul? choose you a man for you, and let him come down to me. If he be able to fight with me, and to kill me, then will we be your servants: but if I prevail against him, and kill him, then shall ye be our servants. The Philistine said, I defy the armies of Israel this day; give me a man, that we may fight together. When Saul and all Israel heard those words, they were dismayed and greatly afraid.

Now David was the son of Jesse; he (Jesse) had eight sons: David was the youngest: the three eldest followed Saul. But David went and returned from Saul to feed his father's sheep at Bethlehem. The Philistine drew near morning and evening, and presented himself forty days.

Jesse said unto David his son, Take now for thy brethren (brothers) an ephah (roughly eight gallons) of this parched corn and these ten loaves, and run to the camp to thy brethren; carry these ten cheeses unto the captain, and look how thy brethren fare.

David rose up early in the morning, and left the sheep with a keeper, and went as Jesse had commanded him; and he came to the trench, as the host was going forth to the fight, and shouted for the battle. Israel and the Philistines had put the battle in array, army against army. David ran into the army, and came and saluted his brethren. As he talked with them, behold, there came up the champion, Goliath, out of the armies of the Philistines, and spake according to the same words: and David heard them. All the men of Israel, when they saw the man, fled from him.

The men of Israel said, Have ye seen this man that is come up? surely to defy Israel is he come up: and it shall be, that the man who killeth him, the king will enrich him with great riches, and will give him his daughter, and make his father's house free in Israel. David spake to the men that stood by him, saying, Who is this un-circumcised Philistine, that he should defy the armies of the living God?

Eliab his eldest brother heard when he spake unto the men; and Eliab's anger was kindled against David, and he said, Why camest thou down hither? and with whom hast thou left those few sheep in the wilderness? I know thy pride, and the naughtiness of thine heart; for thou art come down that thou mightest see the battle. David said, What have I now done? Is there not a cause?

When the words were heard which David spake, they rehearsed them (repeated them) before Saul: and he sent for him.

David said to Saul, Let no man's heart fail because of him; thy servant will go and fight with this Philistine. Saul said to David, Thou are not able to go against this Philistine to fight with him: for thou are but a youth, and he a man of war from his youth. David said unto Saul, Thy servant kept his father's sheep, and there came a lion, and a bear, and took a lamb out of the flock: I went out after him, and smote him, and delivered it out of his mouth: and when he arose against me, I caught him by his beard, and smote him, and slew him. Thy servant slew both the lion and the bear: and this uncircumcised Philistine shall be as one of them, seeing he hath defied the armies of the living God. David said moreover, The Lord that delivered me out of the paw of the lion, and out of the paw of the bear, he will deliver me out of the hand of this Philistine. Saul said unto David, Go, and the Lord be with thee.

David took his staff in his hand, and chose him five smooth stones out of the brook, and put them in a shepherd's bag which he had; and his sling was in his hand: and he drew near to the Philistine. The Philistine came on and drew near unto David; and the man that bare the shield went before him. When the Philistine looked about, and saw David, he disdained him: for he was but a youth, and ruddy, and of a fair countenance. The Philistine said unto David, Am I a dog, that thou comest to me with staves? And the Philistine cursed David by his gods. The Philistine said to David, Come to me, and I will give thy flesh unto the fowls of the air, and to the beasts of the field. Then said David to the Philistine, Thou comest to me with a sword, and with a spear, and with a shield: but I come to thee in the name of the Lord of hosts, the God of the armies of Israel, whom thou hast defied. This day will the Lord deliver thee into mine hand; and I will smite thee, and take thine head from thee; and I will give the carcases of the host of the Philistines this day unto the fowls of the air, and to the wild beasts of the earth; that all the earth may know that there is a God in Israel. All this assembly shall know that the Lord saveth not with sword and spear: for the battle is the Lord's, and he will give you into our hands. It came to pass, when the Philistine arose, and came and drew nigh to meet David, that David hasted, and ran toward the army to meet the Philistine. David put his hand in his bag, and took thence a stone, and slang it, and smote the Philistine in his forehead, that the stone sunk into his forehead; and he fell upon his face to the earth. So David prevailed over the Philistine with a sling and with a stone, and smote the Philistine, and slew him; but there was no sword in the hand of David.

Therefore David ran, and stood upon the Philistine, and took his sword, and drew it out of the sheath thereof, and slew him, and cut off his head therewith. When the Philistines saw their champion was dead, they fled. David took the head of the Philistine, and brought it to Jerusalem.

As David returned from the slaughter of the Philistine, Abner (Saul's military captain) took him, and brought him before Saul with the head of the Philistine in his hand. Saul said to him, Whose son art thou, thou young man? David answered, I am the son of thy servant Jesse the Bethlehemite.

Jack LaLanne

For over sixty years, Jack has been changing individual lives and society as a whole through his teachings, which show people how to be healthier and feel better through vigorous exercise and proper nutrition. Known as the "Godfather of Fitness," he has often dramatized his message by performing extraordinary feats of physical strength and endurance.

At first glance, any comparison of the story of David and Goliath with the larger-than-life Jack LaLanne might seem to put Jack in Goliath's shoes. After all, even though he is not terribly tall, he is muscular and has performed physical feats that have astounded the world. But actually, Jack sees himself more in the role of David.

When he was a boy of fourteen, Jack was a completely different person. He describes himself then as a "junk food junkie" who was thirty pounds underweight. He admits, "I was suicidal. I couldn't stand the terrific headaches I was having every day, being ridiculed by all my classmates. Even the girls used to beat me up in school. I was the brunt of all the attacks."

His personal epiphany came during a health lecture he

attended. The speaker talked about how exercise and a healthful vegetarian diet would change his life for the better. "That night, after hearing that lecture, I went strict vegetarian," Jack recalls. "I cut out all white flour, white sugar, all man-processed, emasculated foods. I joined the Berkeley, California, YMCA, and the rest is history. My life was saved because I went to that health lecture."

The change was quick and dramatic. He went from being the victim of his classmates' abuse to captain of the football team in his senior year. He was so eager to share the benefits he had found, that while he was still in high school, he opened his first gym. There, Jack offered nutritional advice along with comprehensive exercise programs that included weight lifting.

But now, he was being ridiculed by a different group of people—doctors. "Doctors were completely against all this back then because of ignorance," Jack states emphatically. "They knew nothing about nutrition, they knew nothing about vitamins and minerals in those days. And, absolutely, it was forbidden for women to work out with the weights. It was forbidden for older people to work out with the weights, and forbidden for athletes to work out with the weights." Jack says doctors at the time were warning people that women who worked out with weights would develop masculine bodies, older people would die of heart attacks, and athletes would become muscle-bound.

"The doctors were against me, the coaches were against me—everybody!" Jack adds with amazement, "I was a nut! I was a crackpot! Boy, I'm telling you, it was really tough. I had to prove myself just like David. Everybody was dead against everything I was doing."

Well, not everybody. Policemen, firemen, and others who understood the value of a strong, healthy body came to his gym, even though some of them feared being ridiculed. But Jack was not about to let them miss out on the exercise they needed. He gave them keys so they could let themselves in late at night to do their workouts.

Still, the establishment Goliath, made up of doctors, coaches, and other professionals, seemed more interested in defeating his ideas than in exploring them. He was like David, Jack says. "That was me. I'm a little nothing and here's the big establishment. They're trying to pound me down, and it is just fortunate that I'm as stubborn as I am, or I'd never have made it." His drive to get his message across had a very simple basis: "If something saved your life, would you be enthusiastic about it?"

As he energetically spread his message, Jack kept an eye out for new ways to educate people. He was the first person to have a nationally syndicated television show on exercise and nutrition. When his program first began, Jack remembers being called names and having people predict he wouldn't last six weeks. They were more than a little wrong. His program grew to the point where it was shown in two hundred markets and lasted an all-time record of thirty-four years.

The more people attacked his ideas, the more Jack fought to get through to them. The more he fought, the more people tried out his ideas and discovered that they worked.

"The more they would do that, the more enthusiastic I would become about my profession. I'm a competitor, boy. I'm not the biggest guy in the world, it's because I tried so hard!" Jack exclaims. Like David, who honed his slingshot skills as a shepherd so effectively that he was able to kill a bear and a lion to protect his sheep, Jack kept working on ways to get his message heard to save human lives.

Having been raised by a devoutly religious mother, Jack looked to the Bible for inspiration on how to be sure people would pay attention to him. He found it in the miracles that Jesus performed.

"Why did Jesus go around when He's on this earth performing all those miracles? To draw attention to His philosophy, right? Why do I do all the feats that I have done? I had to call attention to my philosophy— that this thing I was preaching worked. If it doesn't work for me, it's not going to work for anybody else," he states firmly.

"So one of the first feats that I did, I swam from Alcatraz prison handcuffed. You know it

---

Some of Jack LaLanne's Incredible Feats

Age 42—Set a record of 1,033 push-ups in 23 minutes on the *You Asked for It* television program.

Age 60—Swam from Alcatraz to Fisherman's Wharf in San Francisco, handcuffed—again. This time he was also shackled and towing a thousand-pound boat.

Age 65—Towed sixty-five boats loaded with sixty-five hundred pounds of wood pulp in Lake Ashinoko, Japan. Again, he was handcuffed and shackled.

Age 70—Fighting strong winds and currents, Jack towed seventy boats with seventy people from the Queen's Way Bridge in Long Beach (California) Harbor to the *Queen Mary*, a distance of 1.5 miles. Oh, yes, he was handcuffed and shackled this time too!

was escape-proof, so I put handcuffs on and swam from Alcatraz to San Francisco. That created international attention. I called attention to my philosophy, and every time I did one of these feats, the business picked up 15 or 20 percent nationwide. Incredible!"

The message that Jack takes from the story of David and Goliath is that if you believe in God, believe that you have a job to do that will help people, and are willing to work hard, you can change the world. After all, when Jack started, common knowledge and even medical advice told people to eat diets high in rich foods and avoid strenuous exercise. Today, everyone knows that a lifestyle with a diet low in fat and high in vegetables, paired with a vigorous exercise program, is usually the key to good health.

Like David, Jack has known for most of his life that he has a mission to accomplish. Noting that everyone in Israel's army thought that Goliath could not be defeated, he adds emphatically, "What did David do? It was impossible what he did! For him to go out there and slay that giant, it was impossible, but he made it happen." Jack's impossible feat was to transform himself from a scrawny, suicidal boy to the man whose work has made people around the world healthier and happier.

Jack concludes with advice he wants everyone to take to heart: "Find something you enjoy—and you believe in—then go get it. Get consumed with it. Anything in life is possible if you make it happen!"

Lillian Vernon

Lillian Vernon's name is well-known in America, with one in four households receiving her delightful and remarkably handy mail-order catalogs. In addition to founding and continuing as Chief Executive Officer (CEO) of a company that generates a quarter of a billion dollars in sales annually, Lillian serves on the boards of many nonprofit organizations, including New York's Lincoln Center and the Virginia Opera, as well as the executive committee of City Meals on Wheels and the Board of Overseers of New York University's College of Arts and Sciences. She, too, chose the story of David and Goliath.

Often, the way people view a particular Bible verse or story evolves throughout their lifetime. That certainly has been the case with Lillian Vernon.

As a young child in Leipzig, Germany, she experienced firsthand many of the horrors that were the Holocaust. The adored daughter of a financially and socially prominent family, Lillian recalls the day when her life changed forever. Her brother, Fred, was practicing the piano when the sounds of the beautiful music were shattered by the Nazis' loud pounding at the front door. They wanted the large, comfortable home as their new headquarters. Her family was told to leave.

Not surprisingly, when she read the story of David and Goliath as a child, Lillian equated the giant, Goliath of Gath, with the Nazi thugs. She acknowledges that Goliath "still reminds me of the Nazis—a larger-than-life presence taking advantage of a frightened group of people."

Losing their home was only the beginning of the anguish that the Nazis would cause Lillian and her family. A bright and social child, she found herself being shunned by other children because she was Jewish. The shunning turned violent two years later when a gang of young Nazis chased Fred home one day. They were screaming "Jüde" at him the whole way, and when they arrived at the family's apartment, they viciously threw him down the stairs. Lillian can still close her eyes and see the blood streaming down her brother's face. "Even now," she notes, "when I hear someone yelling, it makes me cringe."

As the Nazi threat grew, Lillian's father decided that it was time to move. First they went to Amsterdam for a few years, and then on to America. Lillian recalls, "For the second time in my childhood, I was forced to leave familiar surroundings and settle in a country where I didn't speak the language. It was during this period that I became a dreamer—very much in the way that David dreamed of serving the king and becoming king himself. I wanted to do something meaningful with my life, but I was just a young girl in a strange land, and there wasn't anyone to encourage me."

Even as they established themselves in their new lives in America, Lillian's family continued to experience difficult times. Her father's lingerie business was not doing as well as hoped, and her mother had to work as a supervisor at his plant. That left young Lillian responsible for doing all the shopping and cooking for the family dinners after she finished her school day. One bright note for her was the time she spent with her beloved brother, Fred, learning the language and customs of America. She especially remembers when she got her first pair of American penny loafers, and she and Fred joked that as long as she had those shoes, she'd never be broke.

While Lillian was now beginning to think of David and how his role in the story related to her, the Goliath character was about to come back into her life in a horrible way. During his sophomore year at City College of New York, Fred was drafted into the U.S. Army. He was shipped to Europe to serve in the Medical Corps, and his frequent letters were a comfort and joy to the family. Then, following the Normandy invasion, the letters stopped. He was listed missing in September 1944, but it wasn't until April 1945 that the family learned he had been killed by a grenade. Goliath, in the guise of the Nazi Army, had found her family again.

Now, Lillian recalls, "I was an only child, and my parents looked to me for support in their loneliness and devastation. All my dreams of going (away) to college, traveling and spreading my wings were thrust aside . . . I thought forever." Somewhere during this difficult time, Lillian admits, "I forgot about the story of David and Goliath."

As often happens, things settled down and life got better. She studied for two years at New York University before she decided to work for her father. In 1949, Lillian and her parents spent a holiday weekend at a resort in

New Jersey. There she met Sam Hochberg, a charming, handsome, and outgoing man who became her husband within the year.

"In 1951, I was a young newlywed expecting my first child," Lillian remembers. "I sat at my yellow Formica kitchen table and once again dreamed. I wanted to earn a little extra money to ease my family's financial concerns, and thought about starting my own business."

This was no small dream at the time. Social attitudes implied that if a woman worked, her husband was an inadequate provider. Pregnant women were expected to spend their time focusing on the upcoming birth. In addition, working during pregnancy was thought to endanger the health of the baby.

"It was during this time that I had the occasion to reread the story of David and Goliath," Lillian continues. "Suddenly, my perception and interpretation of the story changed. I was no longer focusing on the evils of Goliath and his role in the entire tale. Rather, I found myself drawn to David's strength and self-confidence.

"I realized that in my own way, I was like David. I had the same burning desire to succeed; I had the same courage and determination to take a risk. His brothers were his naysayers, yet he persevered. I, too, had to ignore family and friends who tried to discourage me from taking that big step.

"The story of David and Goliath was the motivation I needed to invest $2,000 of our wedding gift money and start my own business by placing a $495 ad in *Seventeen* magazine. I would be the David of mail order, a small person among giants. How could my offer of a personalized handbag and belt compete with the large catalog companies of the day? That didn't seem to matter to me . . . like David, I didn't let fear of failure thwart my actions."

Lillian's idea—pure marketing genius—was monogramming. By offering to put a girl's monogram on the purse and belt she ordered, each girl received something that both blended in with the fashions worn by her peers and at the same time set her apart as someone special. That first advertisement in *Seventeen* resulted in orders for 6,450 belts and bags. A business was born.

"Today, Lillian Vernon Corporation is a success beyond even my wildest dreams," she notes proudly. "I consider David of Bethlehem my inspiration. I even laugh at the irony that I've been referred to as the Queen of Catalogs—after all, David did become king of Israel."

By fearlessly confronting and defeating Goliath, David demonstrated his faith that God could help him overcome any problem. Lillian adds, "Although David is a biblical and historical figure, he can easily serve as a modern-day role model and success story. More people would reach their goals if they had David's tenacity, common sense, and mental strength . . . a lesson all of us can benefit from."

If you would like to receive a Lillian Vernon catalog, call 1-800-285-5555 or visit her web site at http://www.lillianvernon.com

Nehemiah Rebuilds the Jerusalem Wall

Nehemiah 1-6:15

The words of Nehemiah the son of Hachaliah. It came to pass in the month Chisleu, in the twentieth year, as I was in Shushan the palace, that Hanani, one of my brethren, came, he and certain men of Judah; and I asked them concerning the Jews that had escaped, which were left of the captivity, and concerning Jerusalem. They said unto me, The remnant that are left of the captivity there in the province are in great affliction and reproach: the wall of Jerusalem also is broken down, and the gates thereof are burned with fire.

It came to pass, when I heard these words, that I sat down and wept, and mourned certain days, and fasted, and prayed before the God of heaven, and said, I beseech thee, O Lord God of heaven, the great and terrible God, that keepeth covenant and mercy for them that love him and observe his commandments: Let thine ear now be attentive, and thine eyes open, that thou mayest hear the prayer of thy servant, which I pray before thee now, day and night, for the children of Israel thy servants, and confess the sins of the children of Israel, which have sinned against thee: both I and my father's house have sinned. Remember, I beseech thee, the word that thou commandedst thy servant Moses, saying, If ye transgress, I will scatter you abroad among the nations: But if ye turn unto me, and keep my commandments, and do them; though there were of you cast out unto the uttermost part of the heaven, yet will I gather them from thence, and will bring them unto the place that I have chosen to set my name there. O Lord, I beseech thee, let now thine ear be attentive to the prayer of thy servant, and to the prayer of thy servants, who desire to fear thy name: and prosper, I pray thee, thy servant this day, and grant him mercy in the sight of this man. For I was the king's cupbearer.

It came to pass in the month Nisan, in the twentieth year of Artaxerxes the king, that wine was before him: and I took up the wine, and gave it unto the king. Now I had not been beforetime sad in his presence. Wherefore the king said unto me, Why is thy countenance sad, seeing thou art not sick? this is nothing else but sorrow of heart. Then I was very sore afraid, and said unto the king, Let the king live for ever: why would not my countenance be sad, when the city, the place of my fathers' sepulchres (burial vaults) lieth waste, and the gates thereof are consumed with fire? Then the king said unto me, For what dost thou make request? So I prayed to the God of heaven. I said unto the king, If it please the king, and if thy servant have found favour in thy sight, that thou wouldest send me unto Judah, unto the city of my fathers' sepulchres, that I may build it.

The king said unto me, For how long shall thy journey be? and when wilt thou return? So it pleased the king to send me; and I set him a time. Moreover I said unto the king, If it please the king, let letters be given me to the governors beyond the river, that they may convey me over till I come into Judah; and a letter unto Asaph, the keeper of the king's forest, that he may give me timber to make beams for the gates of the palace, and for the wall of the city. The king granted me, according to the good hand of my God upon me. So I came to Jerusalem, and was there three days.

The rulers knew not whither I went, or what I did; neither had I as yet told it to the Jews, nor to the priests, nor to the rest that did the work.

Then I said unto them, Ye see the distress that we are in, how Jerusalem lieth waste, and the gates thereof are burned with fire: come, let us build up the wall of Jerusalem, that we be no more a reproach (suffer disgrace). Then I told them of the hand of my God which was good upon me; as also the king's words that he had spoken unto me. They said, Let us rise up and build. But when Sanballat, Tobiah, and Geshem heard it, they laughed us to scorn, and despised us. Then answered I them, The God of heaven, he will prosper us; therefore we his servants will arise and build: but ye have no portion (share), nor right (claim), nor memorial, in Jerusalem.

(The sections omitted here go into great detail about how Nehemiah organized the men and the work.)

But it came to pass, that when Sanballat, and Tobiah (and many others) heard that the walls of Jerusalem were made up, and that the breaches began to be stopped, then they were very wroth (upset), and conspired all of them together to come and to fight against Jerusalem, and to hinder it. Nevertheless we made our prayer unto our God, and set a watch against them day and night. Our adversaries said, They shall not know, neither see, till we come in the midst among them, and slay them, and cause the work to cease. It came to pass that when the Jews which dwelt by them came, they said unto us ten times, From all places whence ye shall return unto us they will be upon you.

Therefore set I in the lower places behind the wall, and on the higher places, I even set the people after their families with their swords, their spears, and their bows. It came to pass, when our enemies heard that it was known unto us, and God had brought their counsel to nought, that we returned all of us to the wall, everyone unto his work. They which builded on the wall, and they that bare burdens, every one with one of his hands wrought in the work, and

with the other hand held a weapon. Think upon
me, my God, for good, according to all that I
have done for this people.

Now it came to pass when Sanballat, and Tobiah, and Geshem, and the rest of our enemies,
heard that I had builded the wall, and that there
was no breach left therein; that Sanballat and
Geshem sent unto me saying, Come, let us meet
together in some one of the villages in the plain
of Ono. But they thought to do me mischief. I
sent messengers unto them, saying, I am doing
a great work, so that I cannot come down: why
should the work cease, whilst (while) I leave it,
and come down to you? Afterward I came unto
the house of Shemaiah the son of Delaiah the
son of Mehetabeel, who was shut up; and he
said, Let us meet together in the house of God,
within the temple, and let us shut the doors of
the temple: for they will come to slay thee; yea,
in the night will they come to slay thee. I said,
Should such a man as I flee? and who is there,
that, being as I am, would go into the temple to
save his life? I will not go in. And, lo, I perceived
that God had not sent him; but that he pro-
nounced this prophecy against me: for Tobiah
and Sanballat had hired him. My God, think
thou upon Tobiah and Sanballat according to
these their works.

So the wall was finished in the twenty and
fifth day of the month Elul, in fifty and two
days. It came to pass, that when all our enemies

heard thereof, and all the heathen that were about us saw these things, they were much cast down in their own eyes: for they perceived that this work was wrought of our God.

Laurie Beth Jones

Laurie Beth Jones, the best-selling author of Jesus, CEO; The Path; Jesus in Blue Jeans; *and* Grow Something Besides Old, *is president and founder of The Jones Group, an award-winning leadership development firm. She carries out her mission "to recognize, promote, and inspire the divine connection in all of us" through her books, songs, speeches, and consulting work. Her newest book,* The Power of Positive Prophecy: Finding the Hidden Meaning in Everyday Life, *will be in bookstores in the fall of 1999.*

Often simple questions have results that are anything but simple. Just by asking those questions, people open themselves up to changing their lives—or even the whole world. Laurie sees that happen in the story of Nehemiah. She calls it "a fascinating tale of a man in a very good and happy job who asked a simple question, 'How are the brethren doing in my homeland?' He really cared about the answer, and when he heard what was going on, it moved him. It wracked him to his very bones. Then he prayed and decided to do something about it, and boom!

A week later he's on a horse heading away into the unknown."

Laurie's simple question was "What can I do to right this wrong?" She remembers, "It's very similar, in the sense that I was going along with a very successful advertising agency and saw some things I didn't like in business about the way people were being treated and the trend in business to treat people like pawns—see everything as an adversarial role between labor and management. Then when they lifted up Attila the Hun as the ultimate role model for business, I said, 'That's it!' They went over the line, and so I guess in a way you could say I got on my horse and headed into the wilderness to see what I could do about it. That's how my book *Jesus, CEO* came about.

"One thing that was beautiful about the story of Nehemiah, is that many people have an image of the boss as the bad guy, and here was a boss who loved Nehemiah and noticed that he was not doing well emotionally. Then when Nehemiah made a request, he generously gave him everything he asked for. I think that there are many bosses who truly care about the people they employ. They want to help them with their mission and want them to succeed. That has been my experience through my seminars all over the country."

For instance, she recalls one CEO she has worked with who was in the midst of a merger with four other entities. This merger was going to result in the duplication of three thousand jobs, and the CEO was upset at the disruption this could cause to the workers. "He was agonizing over how to let those workers know what value they had given, and to do it in a graceful way, a meaningful way, so that they would not be damaged in their spirits," Laurie says.

"They put a number of plans in place, including a very generous severance package. They made it so that people could, if they wanted, switch jobs within the organizations if they could. They also paid for some of those people to go back to school. I think, as it worked out, only 15 percent of that three thousand actually had to be laid off." Laurie adds that in addition to the benefits to the employees, there was an additional, unexpected benefit for the organization. Even with the stresses that the merger put on the employees who changed jobs, retired, or were laid off, not a single one instituted litigation against the company.

Laurie points out that having a mission to help out does not mean that everything will go smoothly. She says, "Once you get clear about your mission, you're going to have people come up against you. You know, when Nehemiah was just a cupbearer to the king, he didn't have anybody coming against him, he was doing just fine." However, while he was rebuilding the walls of Jerusalem, Nehemiah had a man come to him in disguise, saying that Nehemiah needed to stop what he was doing, but Nehemiah was able to discern that it was his enemies who sent that man.

Nehemiah also had actual physical threats. He handled the threats of attack by having his people work with one hand on their job and the other hand on their weapon.

Laurie has also experienced the flip side—when people come forward to help out a worthwhile project. For Nehemiah, that became apparent when the people came to work on the wall. For Laurie, it was many things: the women who mobbed her after she spoke at a women's conference and said her message was important and had to get out; the agent who came up to her and offered to represent her book; the businesspeople who have embraced her message and are changing the corporate culture in America, one company at a time.

Laurie says of her work and her book *Jesus, CEO,* "I think it helped create a shift in people's thinking." They are discovering they do not have to treat people like pawns in order to be successful, but it is not always easy. "We're in the creative tension zone," she states. "You have to keep your eye on the bottom line, and at the same time, you want to keep your eye on the noble mission. Like Nehemiah's people, you've got to be working with one hand and keeping the other hand on the sword.

"Nehemiah was a great leader because he got all these people to work together to do something physically visible that led to a spiritual result. It wasn't all pie in the sky, 'Let's all change our hearts and wait for the Messiah to come.' It was 'You know what? We can fix this now. We can fix it with the tools that we have, the team that we have, and we're going to rebuild our pride in the process.' "

Nehemiah and Laurie both asked God one little question, "What can I do to make things better?" Each of them used the direction they received to make life better for countless people. What do you think might happen if you asked the same question?

To learn more about Laurie, her work, and her Jesus CEO Foundation, visit her web site at www.lauriebethjones.com or E-mail her at laurie@lauriebethjones.com

The Story of Job

Job 1-42

There was a man in the land of Uz, whose name was Job; and that man was perfect and upright, and one that feared God, and eschewed (avoided) evil. There were born unto him seven sons and three daughters. His substance also was seven thousand sheep, and three thousand camels, and five hundred yoke of oxen, and five hundred she asses, and a very great household; so that this man was the greatest of all the men of the east.

Now there was a day when the sons of God came to present themselves before the Lord, and Satan came also among them. The Lord said unto Satan, Hast thou considered my servant Job, that there is none like him in the earth, a perfect and an upright man, one that feareth God, and escheweth evil? Then Satan answered the Lord, and said, Doth Job fear God for nought? Hast not thou made an hedge about him, and about his house, and about all that he hath on every side? Thou has blessed the work of his hands, and his substance is increased in the land. But put forth thine hand now, and touch all that he hath, and he will curse thee to thy face. The Lord said unto Satan, Behold, all that he hath is in thy power; only upon himself put not forth thine hand. So Satan went forth from the presence of the Lord.

There was a day when there came a messenger unto Job, and said, The oxen were plowing, and the asses feeding beside them: the Sabeans fell upon them and took them away; yea, they have slain the servants with the edge of the sword; and I only am escaped alone to tell thee. While he was yet speaking, there came also another, and said, The fire of God is fallen from heaven, and hath burned up the sheep, and the servants, and consumed them; and I only am escaped alone to tell thee. While he was yet speaking, there came also another and said, The Chaldeans made out three bands, and fell upon the camels, and have carried them away, yea, and slain the servants with the edge of the sword; and I only am escaped alone to tell thee. While he was yet speaking, there came also another, and said, Thy sons and thy daughters were eating and drinking wine in their eldest brother's house: and, behold, there came a great wind from the wilderness, and smote the four corners of the house, and it fell upon them, and they are dead; and I only am escaped alone to tell thee. Then Job arose, and rent (ripped) his mantle (an almost square piece of fabric worn over other clothes), and shaved his head, and fell down upon the ground, and worshipped,

and said, Naked came I out of my mother's
womb, and naked shall return thither; the Lord
gave, and the Lord hath taken away; blessed be
the name of the Lord. In all this Job sinned not,
nor charged God foolishly.

Again there was a day when the sons of God
came to present themselves before the Lord, and
Satan came also among them to present himself
before the Lord. The Lord said unto Satan, Hast
thou considered my servant Job, that there is
none like him in the earth, a perfect and an upright man, one that feareth God, and escheweth
evil? And still he holdeth fast his integrity, although thou movedst me against him, to destroy
him without cause. Satan answered the Lord,
and said, Skin for skin, yea, all that a man hath
will he give for his life. But put forth thine hand
now, and touch his bone and his flesh, and he
will curse thee to thy face. The Lord said unto
Satan, Behold, he is in thine hand; but save his
life.

So went Satan forth from the presence of the
Lord, and smote Job with sore boils from the
sole of his foot unto his crown. He took him a
potsherd (a piece of broken pottery) to scrape
himself withal; and he sat down among the
ashes.

Then said his wife unto him, Dost thou still
retain thine integrity? Curse God, and die. But
he said unto her, Thou speakest as one of the
foolish women speaketh. What? Shall we receive
good at the hand of God, and shall we not re-

ceive evil? In all this did not Job sin with his lips.

Now when Job's three friends heard of all this evil that was come upon him, they came every one from his own place; Eliphaz the Temanite, and Bildad the Shuhite, and Zophar the Naamathite: for they had made an appointment together to come to mourn with him and comfort him. When they lifted up their eyes afar off, and knew him not, they lifted up their voice and wept; and they rent every one his mantle, and sprinkled dust upon their heads (a sign of mourning). So they sat down with him upon the ground seven days and seven nights, and none spake a word unto him: for they saw that his grief was very great.

(Then for several chapters, his friends try to convince Job that God doesn't love him and that he must have sinned to cause these horrible things to happen.)

(Job replies) Lo, mine eye hath seen all this, mine ear hath heard and understood it. What ye know, the same do I know also: I am not inferior unto you. Surely I would speak to the Almighty, and I desire to reason with God. But ye are forgers of lies, ye are all physicians of no value. O that ye would altogether hold your peace! and it should be your wisdom. Hear now my reasoning, and hearken to the pleadings of my lips. Will ye speak wickedly for God? and talk deceitfully for him? Shall not his excellency make you afraid? and his dread fall upon you?

Hold your peace, let me alone, that I may speak, and let come on me what will. Though he slay me, yet will I trust in him: but I will maintain mine own ways before him. He also shall be my salvation: for an hypocrite shall not come before him. Hear diligently my speech, and my declaration with your ears. Behold now, I have ordered my cause; I know that I shall be justified. Only do not two things unto me: then will I not hide myself from thee. Withdraw thine hand far from me: and let not thy dread make me afraid. Then call thou, and I will answer: or let me speak, and answer thou me. How many are mine iniquities and sins? make me to know my transgression and my sin. (There is a break of twenty-five chapters here. It is mostly Job's discussions with his friends.)

Then the Lord answered Job out of the whirlwind, and said, Where wast thou when I laid the foundations of the earth? declare, if thou hast understanding. Shall he that contendeth with the Almighty instruct him? he that reproveth God, let him answer it.

Then Job answered the Lord, and said, Behold, I am vile; what shall I answer thee? I will lay mine hand upon my mouth. Once I have spoken; but I will not answer: yea, twice; but I will proceed no further.

Then answered the Lord unto Job out of the whirlwind, and said, Wilt thou also disannul (completely cancel) my judgment? wilt thou condemn me that thou mayest be righteous?

Hast thou an arm like God? or canst thou thunder with a voice like him? Deck thyself now with majesty and excellency; and array thyself with beauty.

Then Job answered the Lord, and said, I know that thou canst do every thing, and that no thought can be withholden from thee. Who is he that hideth counsel without knowledge? therefore have I uttered that I understood not; things too wonderful for me, which I knew not. Hear, I beseech (beg) thee, and I will speak: I have heard of thee by the hearing of the ear: but now mine eye seeth thee. Wherefore I abhor myself, and repent in dust and ashes.

And the Lord turned (ended) the captivity of Job: also the Lord gave Job twice as much as he had before. So the Lord blessed the latter end of Job more than his beginning: for he had fourteen thousand sheep, and six thousand camels, and a thousand yoke of oxen, and a thousand she asses. He had also seven sons and three daughters. After this lived Job an hundred and forty years, and saw his sons, and his sons' sons, even four generations. So Job died, being old and full of days.

Robert David Hall

Character actor Robert Hall is familiar to millions for his television and film work. L.A. Law viewers will remember him as Judge Swaybill; Life Goes On viewers, who knew him as Mr. Mott, will easily recognize him in some of his more current guest star roles on many shows, including Brooklyn South, Touched by an Angel, and Promised Land. Robert has also had important character roles in many movies, including Starship Troopers and The Negotiator. His personal time is filled with volunteer activities for the Mutual Amputee Aid Foundation and the Boy Scouts, and he serves on the board of the Media Access Office, which promotes positive and realistic portrayal of people with disabilities in the performing arts.

"The story of Job always made me crazy!" exclaims Robert. "Because I could not understand how somebody could go through all those torments and still come out praising God. It took going through what I went through to actually appreciate Job himself in a deeper way."

His early years gave no hint that Robert would ever be focusing on the story of Job, where a man's faith is tested by an apparently endless stream of tragedy, pain, and anguish. One of five children born to a successful U.S. Navy officer and his artistic wife, Robert seemed to lead a charmed life. He studied theater at UCLA; worked at Disneyland, where he won an employee contest to become the announcer for the Christmas Parade; toured the world as a guitar player in a rock and roll band; and became an award-winning disc jockey on KNX-FM radio in Orange County, California. In the late 1960s and well into the 1970s, he led a life that many only dreamed about.

The event that changed his life began on a most promising day in July 1978. "I had a 1967 Volkswagen that I was going to sell and I was going to buy my first new car," Robert remembers. "A fellow had bought my Volkswagen and I washed and waxed it and was driving to Long Beach to pick up my money and give him my car. I was pretty excited.

"It was about two in the afternoon. A drunk truck driver was steering an eighteen-wheeler south on the San Diego Freeway. I was driving north. He lost control of this huge truck and ran head-on into me. I was in the wrong place at the wrong time. Volkswagens generally lose when they run up against an eighteen-wheel truck.

"I was trapped underneath the wreckage of the truck, and no one knew I was inside this mess because the freeway had turned into a chaotic situation. I was wide awake and banged up pretty badly. About ten minutes later, my gas tank exploded and I was trapped in the fire underneath the truck. I was certain I was going to die physically that day.

"I'm no expert on how people die. I just know what I went through. I've always been very, very hard on myself—competitive and always wanting to move up to the next level; be a better musician, a better radio person, a better actor, things like that. When I knew that I was going to die, it was like a sense of forgiveness passed over me. I realized that I had done the best I could do, and I had a great sense of peace. I think I came to a point of actually accepting what seemed like the inevitable."

Robert continues, "I had not really yelled up to that point. I could hear all of the commotion outside, and one of the things I heard was a policeman. People were terrified that the gas tank on the big truck was going to explode." While he had begun yelling for help, Robert was still mainly focusing calmly on the thoughts in his mind: his late mother, his friends, even a picture of Jesus he had colored in Vacation Bible School as a child. His reverie was shattered when he heard the policeman who was trying to move people away from the flames shout, "Forget about him!" referring to Robert, who then *really* began to scream. "I'm Welsh and Irish and have a big, loud voice. I believe that was probably the loudest I ever yelled in my life."

Instantly, a retired welder from the Los Angeles city schools reached into his truck and grabbed a big fire extinguisher. He and another man jammed it down into the flames and fought back the fire to the point where the two of them and the policeman were able to get a chain around part of the demolished VW and drag it out so Robert could be rescued.

"I'd been in the fire for about ten minutes, and I was burned quite severely, over about 65 percent of my body," Robert recalls. When they finished pulling him out of the flaming car, the gravity of the situation became immediately apparent when he looked down at his lap. "I looked down and saw my brand new blue jeans were black and I knew something was wrong." Paramedics quickly got him to the nearby U.C. Irvine burn ward.

"That's when the real journey began," Robert states. "And that's my fascination with the book of Job. Without trying to aggrandize the experience I went through, I spent three months in the burn ward as a critical burn care patient."

Robert's right leg was too damaged to save and had to be amputated that first night. His left leg came off in cruel stages. First he lost the fight to save his toes and they had to be amputated. After hope faded for saving his foot, it went. His doctors worked feverishly to save his ankle— and lost. Finally his calf had to be amputated. "That was the hellacious thing about being in the burn ward, the hoping that you could keep a leg and then watching it slowly go," he remembers sadly.

An especially painful treatment that many burn victims must undergo is debridement. It involves soaking in a large tank and having dead tissue removed to make healing possible. "There's no morphine or anything else that can ease that pain," he says. "You think strange thoughts when you're going through this."

One thought that kept coming back was the Bible story of Job. "Job, as I understood the story, was a good man, respected. He had seven sons and three daughters. He was a wise man, helpful, wealthy, did good things with his wealth and always honored God and paid obeisance. Then God and the Devil got into a pissing match. Satan said to God, 'Sure he's good, but that's because you surrounded him with all this comfortable, happy stuff. All this money.

All these good children. He wouldn't love you unconditionally the way you say he does if he didn't have these things.' And God says, 'Oh, yeah?' Then Satan goes down and thieves steal Job's herd. The house caves in on all his children and they die. Job is pretty unhappy about it, but still honors and loves God. Satan says, 'Well, if he was suffering himself . . .' and God says he can do anything to Job but kill him. So Satan goes down and Job has boils and sores and every misery you can possibly imagine. Much like, I thought much later, the burn ward. It's like, could Job have been the guy lying in the bed next to me in the burn ward? I don't know, but it made some sense."

During his sufferings, Job was visited by many friends who often tried to explain why these horrible things had happened to him and said that he should curse God for it. Robert had many friends visit him, and observed that they had different ways of handling his situation. Some, like Job's friends, were ready to curse God for letting this happen; others were praising God for sparing his life.

Robert notes that even the most caring people often make one of the mistakes that Job's friends made—trying too hard to find a reason for what has happened. "Sometimes just sitting and listening or just being there is more important than trying to explain," Robert says. "This is where Job's friends let him down. Job just needed somebody to sit there with him and bring him a glass of water and shut up."

Robert goes back to the thought that God allowed Job to suffer and says, "I was mad at God for allowing Job to be tested. If you're God, don't you KNOW what he's like? Don't you KNOW if he's a good person? But the whole point of the book of Job, and this is a hard one for me, is that as smart as we are, as many experiences as we have, as artistic and brilliant as we are—and I think we as a people are—there are some unknowable things and some powerful things that we have to let go of—and I don't like letting go. Job saw God's power and realized that he would not understand everything about his test, and he had to let go of some of it. So ultimately I, too, had to let go."

Job passes the test and continues to love and praise God. In time, he has ten more children and double the wealth he had before the test began. Robert, too, has seen blessings and opportunities that he would never have sought or recognized before the fire. He finds himself being much more open emotionally to what people have on their minds. He also finds himself reaching out to support new amputees through the Mutual Amputee Aid Foundation, and to help performers who have disabilities break into the entertainment industry through his work with the Media Access Office.

While unlike Job, Robert did not get back everything he'd lost, his life is good personally and professionally. He is able to walk well on prosthetic legs, play his guitar (a passion Robert developed after seeing Roy Rogers play in a movie when he was a child), work in an industry he loves, and be an active parent to his son, Andrew Evan Hall.

Is he a more spiritual person because of his experiences? Robert says thoughtfully, "I think I've always been a spiritual person. This loving God is not the easiest thing, and I think it's what Job teaches us. It's not all roses and skipping merrily to a beautiful tune in a meadow.

"I believe in God and I believe there's a reason for my

accident, and I want to understand it. I want to have a little bit of peace around the things I can't understand. That's how I'm different. Before, I would not grant myself any peace about the things that made no sense. Job has helped me deal with it."

Job 36:5-6

Behold, God is mighty, and despiseth not any: he is mighty in strength and wisdom. He preserveth not the life of the wicked: but giveth right to the poor.

Erin Moran

The delightful young Joanie of TV's Happy Days *and* Joanie Loves Chachi *has grown into a beautiful and thoughtful woman. Still very much a professional actress, Erin recently guest-starred on* Diagnosis Murder *and was one of the actors who provided voices for the animated film* Magic Pony. *Unfortunately, her real-life growing up was not much like Joanie Cunningham's. She recounts one aspect of the problems she faced and overcame in this story. Look for the whole story in her autobiography, which should be available soon. After talking about her personal struggles, she was asked what she wanted to be sure was in her introduction. Her answer says a lot about how she won her battles: "Glory be to God in the highest!"*

In the story of Job, a good man faces unbelievable tragedy and pain, yet still thanks and praises God for the goodness that he has experienced in his life. Job also asks God to explain why he is suffering, and learns that God's reasons are often unknowable to humans. When Job continues to be faithful even after he realizes that he'll never completely understand, God rewards him for his faith.

For Erin, the two verses she chose hold a whole lot of meaning in a very few words. She states firmly, "God doesn't persecute anyone. He doesn't despise anyone. He loves all his children." Those simple sentences show how far she has come from the young child whose work financially supported her entire family of eight and the teenager who somehow felt responsible when the family broke apart. About that time, she says, "My parents were getting divorced and I didn't understand why. It wasn't because of me. It wasn't my fault. At the time I didn't understand it. I blamed it on me."

Many children whose families experience divorce think that it was somehow their fault. Erin had an added pressure that as a young actress, she had to be accompanied to the set every day by her mother, and to her, that meant her needs had destroyed the family.

During those years, Erin was piling heavy, unattainable expectations on herself, even when others weren't. A school test she did not do well on, an audition where she failed to get the part, all weighed on her and caused her to see herself as a failure.

She describes those times: "A lot of my life, everything was on me. People depended on me for money and all that. There were six kids, so there was a lot of need. We were pretty poor. We frequently had the same food every night. My parents would argue a lot. But then things started to go better as soon as I started working more and I made that little connection. The more I worked, the better things were. But there were still arguments and I would think, 'Oh, my gosh, I must have done something wrong. It must have been me. God is persecuting me. I'm not good enough.' "

The next phrase of these verses, "He is mighty in

strength and wisdom," really helped Erin turn things around. It was a promise she could cling to when her own strength was spent and her own wisdom was not enough to handle the situations she found herself dealing with. Erin freely admits that as she was growing up, her relationship with God, like many people's, was stronger at some times than at others. As she looks back, Erin acknowledges, "God gave me the strength and wisdom. I didn't have much. I had a lot of strength, but only in certain areas like willpower, but strength with my heart and my emotions—and wisdom—that's something I had hardly any of, but I sure did get quite a bit!"

"He preserveth not the life of the wicked" is the next phrase in Erin's verses. She found that God used this phrase to help her let go of a great deal of pain. Like many children, she had times when she wished she had no parents, that they would die. Some of this was normal childhood wishful thinking when things were bad. However, Erin also had to deal with a great deal of animosity from both parents after their divorce. It caused her a great deal of pain, and she found her

Sweet Like Chocolate

After working most of her childhood and early adulthood, Erin took a break from acting for some years, but is raring to come back. She says, "I've always liked acting so much, and it is such a wonderful blessing from God that he gave it to me in the first place, but liking it to boot—it's kind of like chocolate. It's hard to put it down and leave it forever. I really enjoy acting and making people laugh and causing emotions—but mostly laughing. Actually, on *Happy Days,* I really got a kick out of making people laugh. It's such a wonderful feeling!"

mind going back to this topic over and over again. Then she started actually listening to what her parents were fighting about and then taking her problems to God in prayer.

"All that (pain) changed the more I listened and paid attention, especially with what happened with the arguments and the way things were. I listened to God a lot more and got 'No, no, no, you don't want to think that or feel that, because that's wrong. It's not right to think that. It's better to think the best and pray for the best with the worst situation or the worst person in the world. And that's what I did with my parents in every situation, and that's how I made it through, was to think the best and not become bitter over all the bad stuff.'"

The final phrase in Erin's chosen verses is "But [He] giveth right to the poor." Certainly, in Job's situation, God did take note of the fact that he was poor in health, spirit, and earthly goods, and God did make Job's personal world right again.

Erin sees that phrase as both a promise and an opportunity. "If you are poor in your wisdom, or your money, or with anything, you shouldn't look toward God as the one that's causing it," she states. She adds that the circumstances we find ourselves in are often that, just circumstances. "The situation you're in, the way you're feeling, the way you're thinking, where you are. You can change it and make it better. The more positive you feel and think and pray to God to help you, it will change— and it has for me."

Erin also says that there can be parallels between the large and small difficulties people face today and the story of Job. When we are facing any difficulties, it helps to think of them as tests, the way Job was tested. She says that one way to look at it is "All of these things are to make you stronger. It's all a test to see how strong you feel about God and how much you want to make things better. It is God testing you to see your love and your strength for him."

Having overcome incredible personal challenges that she faced at a very young age, Erin says, "I'll never have no faith for God at all, NO WAY! He's given me too much and there's too much of a relationship that we've had throughout my life. I know that there's nothing in my life that could change my faith."

Erin's fans can reach her by E-mail at em-fans@ rocketmail.com. She enjoys hearing from them and tries to answer every letter.

Psalm 91

He that dwelleth in the secret place of the most High shall abide under the shadow of the Almighty. I will say of the Lord, He is my refuge and my fortress: my God; in him will I trust. Surely he shall deliver thee from the snare of the fowler, and from the noisome pestilence. He shall cover thee with his feathers, and under his wings shall thou trust: his truth shall be thy shield and buckler. Thou shalt not be afraid for the terror by night; nor for the arrow that flieth by day; nor for the pestilence that walketh in darkness; nor for the destruction that wasteth at noonday. A thousand shall fall at thy side, and ten thousand at thy right hand; but it shall not come nigh thee. Only with thine eyes shalt thou behold and see the reward of the wicked. Because thou hast made the Lord, which is my refuge, even the most High, thy habitation; there shall no evil befall thee, neither shall any plague come nigh thy dwelling. For he shall give his angels charge over thee, to keep thee in all thy ways. They shall bear thee up in their hands, lest thou dash thy foot against a stone. Thou shalt tread upon the lion and adder: the young lion and the dragon shalt thou trample under feet. Because he hath set his love upon me, therefore will I deliver him: I will set him on high, because he hath known my name. He shall call upon me, and I will answer him: I will be with him in trouble; I will deliver him, and honour him. With long life will I satisfy him, and shew him my salvation.

Wally Amos

"Famous" is the first word that comes to most people's minds when they think of Wally Amos. Wally founded Famous Amos Cookies in 1975 and today serves as spokesman for that company. He is also the founder and chairman of Uncle Wally's producers of healthy fat-free and sugar-free muffins. Wally shares the knowledge he has gained in his tumultuous career through his inspirational speeches and books. His latest is Watermelon Magic. *Wally is especially passionate about the importance of literacy and serves as the national spokesperson for Literacy Volunteers of America and as a board member of the National Center for Family Literacy.*

No one would have blamed Wally if he had given up on his dreams early and settled for whatever came his way. His mother, Ruby, was a domestic, and his father, Wallace, was a laborer in Florida. However, his entrepreneurial spirit was there from the beginning. Even as a child, Wally was creating new businesses, starting with a shoeshine box, little realizing that his entrepreneurial spirit would one day result in winning the President's Award for Entrepreneurial Excellence.

The idea of starting any kind of business terrifies many people. They can worry about the risk so much that they never get started. Wally has found that reading and meditating on Psalm 91 can give him the peace to face the challenges he has found in his life and his work. He says, "I know that God created me, and so if God created me, surely he'll give me whatever I need to live my life."

As a young man, Wally's career took some fascinating turns. After a stint in the U.S. Air Force, he went to work in the supply department of Saks Fifth Avenue, where he rose to executive status in only a few years. When opportunities for career growth were no longer there at Saks, he joined the William Morris Agency and rose in their ranks to become their first black agent. While he was there, Wally assisted in launching the careers of many famous musical artists, including Simon and Garfunkel, the Supremes, and the Temptations.

When show business lost its luster, Wally began thinking of the wonderful chocolate chip cookies his Aunt Della had made when he was a child. He had been making those cookies for clients for years and had found that they opened a lot of doors for him.

Starting his own cookie business was a dream come true. He had learned management skills at Saks, promotional skills as an agent, and had a wonderful recipe and a commitment to make his cookies with only the very best ingredients.

Wally says, "Life is never really what it seems, it's always more!" His cookie business took off like a rocket, and "Famous Amos" really did become famous.

During this time, Wally first became aware of Psalm 91 during a church service. It spoke to his heart, and he found himself reading and rereading it. Some of its vivid images were especially important, including "under his wings shall thou trust," because of the feeling of safety and protection it gives him.

The phrase "For he shall give his angels charge over thee" reminds him of the sense he had always had that he was being watched over. When asked if he's ever had a sensation of angels watching over him, Wally replies, "Not necessarily angels, but there are many moments when I've had a sense that I was protected by something greater than me, by some wonderful, positive force in the universe. I was thinking about people in my life who had really loved and been supportive of me while they were living, and now that they are no longer living, perhaps they have all banded together and are really supporting me.

"There were so many times in the early stages of Famous Amos when there was no question that Aunt Della or somebody was looking over my shoulder, was really protecting me. There were so many close calls and good always came from all of them, so I thought that Aunt Della was one of my guardian angels. And my mother, who died in 1994, I know that she's up there doing everything possible to make sure that her son succeeds."

By the mid-1980s Wally's cookie company was a popular success with sales of more than $10 million. Unfortunately, his lack of experience as the head of a large company resulted in business problems and he was forced to relinquish ownership—including the use of the "Famous Amos" name he had created for himself. (He returned as company spokesperson in 1999).

During this extremely difficult time, Wally often thought

back to Psalm 91. "It absolutely helped. There were several times during all of that, that I would review the 91st Psalm and it was very comforting. It was very supportive. I mean, you have to believe it though; it's just words otherwise."

This psalm is something that Wally feels very deeply about. It talks to him about the ways that by trusting God, he can know he is always being protected. "I will say of the Lord, He is my refuge and my fortress: my God; in him will I trust" is especially important. "I don't perceive that God is a person, a long-bearded guy who's up there dispensing favors, or withholding favors," says Wally thoughtfully. "For me, God is a positive force, an energy, spirit, that permeates everything. So when I read that, I think in terms of the goodness of the universe. I trust the goodness of life. I trust the life that is in the palm fronds as I look out my window, and know that the same life that inhabits the palm fronds, inhabits me. As I see the birds flitting about, I know that the same life that inhabits the birds inhabits me. I trust because that is my essence, which cannot be defined. I mean, God cannot be defined. The sense of exactly what God is, as soon as you pigeon-hole it with a narrow human definition, you limit it."

Even without being able to define God, Wally makes his faith central to who he is and what he does. "My faith is extended to everything that I do. It supports everything. It's involved in everything that I do, because it is the foundation of my belief system. It helps me have a passion for people I work with (especially in his literacy work) and not see them as victims, but see their magnificence, and to know that the same God that supports and nourishes me, supports and nourishes them. Without my faith, I cannot be effective in any of the work that I do."

Wally is active in several organizations that help people achieve literacy. He says, "It's very important to be able to read, perhaps more so today than ever before. Everything is computer-driven and information-driven these days, so it becomes really vital to be able to read. Even on a basic level, just to go shopping to buy food for yourself. If you can't read, you can't do that. I've heard so many horror stories of people buying food because of the pictures on the products and getting home and having lemon detergent instead of lemon juice because all they can do is identify the picture. Reading is absolutely vital to one's well-being. I've met several gentlemen who've been incredibly successful financially who are unable to read or write, but it always haunted them. They always felt that a part of them was missing."

On a personal level, Wally is grateful that he's always been able to read, because it enables him to internalize the material he reads and make it a part of himself. He believes that when people can read for themselves, it allows them to get the most in all areas of life, including reading the Bible and other books to help them get through trying times.

When asked what he would tell people who are experiencing difficult times, he says, "I'd tell them to read the 91st Psalm thoroughly many times. To internalize it. To trust this and to live it. Don't question it. Don't analyze it. Just do what it says. Information gained has no value until you apply it. So my message to them is to suggest that they apply the 91st Psalm to their life and see if it doesn't work. I mean, it really does! I *know* it does. If it works for me, it will work for anyone. That's the bottom line."

Proverbs 22:6

Train up a child in the way he should go: and
when he is old, he will not depart from it.

Dale Evans Rogers

~~≈≈~~

Beloved by generations as the Queen of the West, Dale has brought joy into the lives of millions of people through her performances on the Roy Rogers Show. *Yet her acting and singing are only a few of her many talents. Dale is an accomplished musical composer, best-selling author, and gifted speaker whose work has brought countless people to a closer relationship with God through her personal appearances.*

Sometimes a Bible verse is such an integral part of a person's life, it has a meaning that stretches from one generation to another. That is the way Dale has experienced her verse, "Train up a child in the way he should go: and when he is old, he will not depart from it." It has resonated throughout her life.

Dale remembers how when she was a young actress, her mother claimed (took it to her heart as a promise from God) the verse for her. Talking about those years, she remembers, "I never really got away from the Lord. I just didn't pay any attention to Him. To what He said.

"My mother was not really excited about my being in show business, you know. Her sister would say to her,

'What's going to happen to Frances?' That's my real name, Frances Octavia Smith. And my mother would say, 'She will come back, for the Bible does not lie. The Bible says to train up a child in the way he should go, and when he is old, he will not depart from it. It does not say he might not try his wings a bit, getting to be old.'

"God really answered her faithfulness and he let her see me come back full circle to my faith, and she saw it for a number of years, from 1947 until our bicentennial year, when she died."

Children have always played a big role in Dale's life. At the time of her wedding to her television costar, Roy Rogers, on December 31, 1947, Dale had a son from a previous marriage, and Roy was a widower with three young children. Over the years, they adopted four more and gave birth to their daughter Robin Elizabeth.

Robin was born with multiple handicaps including Down Syndrome, and died just before her second birthday. Her brief but very special life is the subject of Dale's best-selling book, *Angel Unaware*.

With a house filled with children, Dale made sure that helping them get to know God was a priority. "I took them—I didn't send them—to Sunday school and church. I went too," she states.

It saddens her to see families who let other priorities get in the way of teaching their children about God—and especially when the parents neglect to teach their children about God at all, on the assumption that the children can decide about God and religion when they are adults. "There's too much that crowds the mind in the interim and they might not get faith," she states firmly. "So they have to have an example set before them. I believe you must take your children to Sunday school and church."

But teaching a child about values and morals is more than just taking them to religious services. It is the way they see their parents behaving on a day-to-day basis. "Their little minds are so fresh and so easily impressed, and through the years you never know what you say that will come back to a child later, when they're an adult," Dale states.

Children can tell when an adult, especially a parent, is telling them to behave one way while doing something entirely different. It doesn't do much good to tell children how important it is to avoid smoking so they will be healthy, if they see you lighting up. It doesn't do any good to tell them to be honest if they see you pocket too much change from the store clerk or hear you brag about cheating on your taxes.

Everyone faces those moments when they have to decide whether to do the thing they want to do or set the right example for their children. Dale faced exactly that kind of problem when she was returning home from a Hawaiian vacation with four of her children, who were very young at the time.

"I was just entranced by the wonderful fruit, the fresh pineapple, mangoes, all those things. They have a small, fat banana over there and it was the best banana you've ever tasted in your life. I determined that I was going to bring some home.

"Now, you're not supposed to bring fresh fruit out of Hawaii. I was going through the line, getting ready to get on the plane, and the fellow says, 'Do you have anything? Are you carrying any fresh fruit?'

"I was going to say no. I had the bananas hidden in my big sun hat and I had it on the top of my head with the little bananas inside. I had two wonderful women who worked for me in the home, and I was going to bring these bananas to them and let them taste what a *real* banana tasted like."

Dale continues, "I was going to tell him no, and then I saw my children standing right behind me. I looked at them and I thought, I can't do this in front of my children. So I said, 'Sir, I have some bananas on the top of my head.' The children laughed and he laughed. I said, 'Sir, I am a Christian. These are my children, and I cannot lie in front of them.' So I gave him the bananas."

Dale adds that there are times when parents need to take a stand and insist that their children learn right from wrong. It can be as difficult for the parents as it is for the child, and sometimes parents are tempted to let things slide and take the easy way out. "They want to make their children happy," Dale notes. "But they don't have tough love with their children. Having tough love means that you have to deny some of the things they think they want to do and you know that it's wrong. You know they will pay for it. So therefore you have to take your stand in front of your children, even if it makes for upset."

One area where many families take a stand is on what kind of television programs their children watch. It can be tough to be the parents who do not let their children watch the programs their friends are seeing because those programs have violence, adult themes, or other content that is not appropriate for children. Dale and Roy worked hard to present wholesome values on their program, the *Roy Rogers Show,* which ran from 1950 to 1957. In fact,

Roy never shot anyone—just the guns out of their hands—on his program. He was a crack shot and often gave demonstrations at rodeos.

Dale also helped reinforce positive values in the program and through her music. As a songwriter, she is probably best known for writing the show's theme song, "Happy Trails to You." One of her other songs is also well known to a generation of fans, many of whom have taught it to their children. "We happened to need a little song for a little girl in this one episode," Dale remembers. "Her father was falsely accused of theft, and I wrote that song for her to sing. The whole cast sang it with her."

That song is "The Bible Tells Me So." In case you've forgotten a few of the words or never learned this delightful melody, with Dale's permission, here it is!

The Bible Tells Me So
by Dale Evans

Have faith, hope and char - i - ty,_ That's the way to live suc -

cess - ful - ly._ How do I know? The Bi - ble tells me so._

Do good to your en - e - mies_ And the Bless - ed Lord you'll

sure - ly please_ How do I know? The Bi - ble tells me so._

Don't wor - ry 'bout to - mor - row, just be real good to -

day. The Lord is right be - side you, He'll guide you all the

way. Have faith, hope and char - i - ty,_ That's the way to live suc -

cess - ful - ly._ How do I know? The Bi - ble tells me so._

Jonah and the Whale

Jonah 1-3:3

Now the word of the Lord came unto Jonah the son of Amittai, saying Arise, go to Nineveh, that great city, and cry against it; for their wickedness is come up before me. But Jonah rose up to flee unto Tarshish from the presence of the Lord, and went down to Joppa; and he found a ship going to Tarshish: so he paid the fare thereof, and went down into it, to go with them unto Tarshish from the presence of the Lord.

But the Lord sent out a great wind into the sea, and there was a mighty tempest in the sea, so that the ship was like to be broken. Then the mariners were afraid, and cried every man unto his god, and cast forth the wares (merchandise being shipped) that were in the ship into the sea, to lighten it of them. But Jonah was gone down into the sides of the ship; and he lay, and was fast asleep. So the shipmaster came to him, and said unto him, What meanest thou, O sleeper? arise, call upon thy God, if so be that God will think upon us, that we perish not. They said every one to his fellow, Come, and let us cast lots (a gambling technique used to make a determination), that we may know for whose cause this evil is upon us. So they cast lots, and the lot fell upon Jonah. Then they said unto him, Tell us, we pray thee, for whose cause this evil is upon us; What is thine occupation? and whence comest thou? what is thy country? and of what people art thou? And he said unto them, I am an Hebrew; and I fear the Lord, the God of heaven, which hath made the sea and the dry land. Then were the men exceedingly afraid, and said unto him, Why has thou done this? For the men knew that he fled from the presence of the Lord, because he had told them.

Then said they unto him, What shall we do unto thee, that the sea may be calm unto us? for the sea wrought, and was tempestuous. He said unto them, Take me up, and cast me forth into the sea; so shall the sea be calm unto you: for I know that for my sake this great tempest is upon you. So they took up Jonah, and cast him forth into the sea: and the sea ceased from her raging. Then the men feared the Lord exceedingly, and offered a sacrifice unto the Lord, and made vows.

Now the Lord had prepared a great fish to swallow up Jonah. Jonah was in the belly of the fish three days and three nights.

Then Jonah prayed unto the Lord his God out of the fish's belly, and said, I cried by reason of mine affliction unto the Lord, and he heard me; out of the belly of hell cried I, and thou heardest my voice. For thou hadst cast me into the deep, in the midst of the seas; and the floods compassed me about: all thy billows and thy waves passed over me. Then I said, I am cast out of thy sight; yet I will look again toward thy holy temple. The waters compassed me about, even to the soul: the depth closed me round about, the weeds were wrapped about my head. I went down to the bottoms of the mountains; the earth with her bars was about me for ever: yet has thou brought up my life from corruption, O Lord my God. When my soul fainted within me I remembered the Lord: and my prayer came in unto thee, into thine holy temple. They that observe lying vanities forsake their own mercy. But I will sacrifice unto thee with the voice of thanksgiving; I will pay that that I have vowed. Salvation is of the Lord.

The Lord spake unto the fish, and it vomited out Jonah upon the dry land. The word of the Lord came unto Jonah the second time, saying, Arise, go unto Nineveh, that great city, and preach unto it the preaching that I bid thee. So Jonah arose, and went unto Nineveh, according to the word of the Lord.

Lauraine Snelling

~~~

Best-selling author Lauraine Snelling has over thirty-five titles in print with approximately one million books sold. Younger readers cannot get enough of her two series of novels about horses, including the Golden Filly *series about horse racing and the* High Hurdle *series about jumping. Adult readers are drawn to her historical and romance novels that chronicle the lives and adventures of the settlers who built America, including the* Dakota *series and* Red River of the North *series. Lauraine is also in demand as a speaker at conferences and workshops.*

One of the great things about fiction writers is that they are often the best storytellers. Lauraine tells the story of Jonah this way:

"Jonah is a prophet, and he is called to go to Nineveh to tell the people that God said, 'If you don't shape up, I'm going to destroy the city with you in it.'

"Jonah says, 'Excuse me, but I don't want to do that!' and God says, 'Go!' and Jonah says, 'No!'

"So Jonah gets on a boat and he's going to run away from God. The boat hits a big storm and Jonah knows that God's after him. So he tells the sailors, 'Just throw me overboard. It's my fault that you're all going to drown because of this storm.'

"So the sailors throw him overboard and the storm stops immediately. Then Jonah's swallowed by a whale. He is in the belly of the whale for three days. I love it because things are kinda fishy—smelling kinda fishy by then. Then the whale burps him up on the sandbank and Jonah says, 'All right, already, I'll go to Nineveh!' So he goes to Nineveh, tells them they have to repent or God's going to destroy the city, and they do.

"Now that's a slightly different story than you're going to get from the Bible, but that's my version," Lauraine says. "What I like about Jonah is that he's a chronic crybaby. He really is. He's a crybaby. He's a coward. He didn't want to go to Nineveh. He's stubborn. He's obnoxious. I mean, he goes out and tries to run away from God, and yet in the end, God uses him anyway and that's the part that's so incredible to me!

"There are so many times in my life that I feel like I'm a crybaby, and a coward, and I don't like what God's doing, and I don't want to do it. I try to explain it to Him just like Jonah. Jonah's right before God, right in His face, saying 'I don't want to do this, I don't like it, I don't think it's fair, blah, blah, blah,'—and yet God uses him anyway.

"To me that is an absolutely incredible story because not all of the men of the Bible were great people. The great men and the great women were real human beings, and Jonah was one who was really, really human. He tried running and he tried running. I tried running and I tried running and it doesn't work. God just keeps coming after you until you say, 'That's it. OK. Fine. Let's do what you want to do anyway.' "

Like many people, Lauraine first heard the story of Jonah as a child. She recalls, "I can remember as a little kid singing about Jonah and the whale, and I just thought this guy getting swallowed by the whale was the funniest thing in the whole world. I mean, come on, I didn't know what whales were. I didn't know how big they were, but I remember thinking as a little kid, 'I wonder if he could stand up in there?' As I got older and realized the pure motivation for Jonah, I liked the story even more."

Lauraine says she definitely identifies with Jonah, even more so since she and her husband moved to rural southern California. She remembers, "Wayne (her husband) says we're going to move to this small town hundreds of miles from where we were living and I said, 'No, we're not!' I fought that tooth and nail. Yet I still had to just turn around and give it up because I knew, as I listened and paid attention, that God was calling us to go there. I really believed that, but I was not happy with it and I whined and I cried, and I screamed at God and I did all kinds of things. Yet, now I can see God doing good things, because we moved there."

One of the blessings she has seen is a whole new level of energy to invest in her writing. "We're out in the country again, and I love being out in the county. Having my own yard, a place of my own, having the mountains around us, all of that has made my writing very strong. Several times I have really felt that God is saying, 'I have done this for you.' "

Another blessing was the gift of health insurance. Poor health had been keeping her husband from working at their old home, and as a result, they had lost their health insurance. His health improved so much in the new climate that he was able to work, and became covered under his employer's health insurance policy only months before a new health crisis put him in a hospital. Even now, as he works to regain his health and return to his job, the health insurance continues to be a blessing that smooths his rehabilitation.

However, before the health insurance, there was a moment where Lauraine knew that no matter how Jonah-like she had been with her reluctance to move, God had really planned it for her benefit all along. "Years ago, when I was at dinner at a friend's home, there was a little quail rooster crowing on the fence," she recalls. "My fleeting thought was, 'Someday, God, I'd like to live where I have a little quail rooster crowing.' The day the real estate agent showed me the house we ended up purchasing, we stepped out on the front porch, and over on one of the bushes was a little quail rooster crowing. Right then, it was like I knew. That was my little sign from God that said, 'See, I am in control and I am taking care of you.' "

To Lauraine, the story of Jonah is much, much more than a children's story where a man gets eaten by a whale and "burped" up on a sandbank. "Now it's the story about a man," Lauraine states. "A man of God, because Jonah was already one of the prophets. A man of God turning his back and trying to run and still being used by God. That's the thing I keep coming back to. We can be such idiots and God still uses us. I like that. It's very comforting."

St. Matthew 5:16

Let your light so shine before men (meaning all people), that they may see your good works, and glorify your Father which is in heaven.

Thomas Kinkade

Renowned as the "Painter of Light," award-winning artist Thomas Kinkade is the most successful painter of our time. His paintings appear to glow with a light from within and evoke warm and comforting feelings in those who view them.

Reflecting thoughtfully about his early years as a painter, Thomas Kinkade remarks, "I had never associated my faith directly with whatever talents I had. I just thought, 'I want to go out there and make my living painting!' I would describe my art as something I did for my own enjoyment.

"In fact, this was reinforced in college. I remember so many art teachers who would say, 'Your art is all about you. It doesn't matter if someone appreciates it. Whether they understand it. Whether they like it. What matters is you do it for you.' I kind of bought into that to some degree."

But Kinkade was finding no personal satisfaction in art for self-fulfillment only. He was seeing that in many ways, all his work to develop his talent was only leading to a commercial treadmill that offered no satisfaction to him.

The crisis of confidence he was experiencing came to a wonderful and somewhat surprising climax when he was only twenty-two years old. "I was in a little church in Pasadena. I walked in and knew that the Holy Spirit was tugging at my heart," Kinkade remembers. "I didn't really have any interest in making some dramatic statement, and yet the Holy Spirit really, really impressed on me to go up for prayer, and this led me to the Lord right on the spot! I had known the Lord as a child, but not in a real personal way.

"When I turned my life over to Christ, I couldn't believe that my art was all about me anymore. It didn't strike me as a sound form of justification for creating art. At that point, my art went from self-focused to other-focused. The light came in. It was just unbelievable."

From his earliest days as a painter, it had been apparent that Kinkade had a special gift for painting so that light seemed to radiate from his work. After committing himself and his work to the Lord, the light seemed to shine through his work even more. People started calling him the "Painter of Light," not in a religious sense originally, but because the light effects in his paintings were so re-markable.

Kinkade came to his favorite Bible verse not through a major revelation complete with fireworks, but through a slow and reflective process of personal study.

Kinkade was only six years old when his father left and his mother, Mary Anne, shouldered the responsibility of raising three children on her own. A woman of faith, she struggled to bring up her children with a knowledge of God's love and grace, but the message didn't really "take" with Kinkade. "I had a seminal form of faith all through high school, being raised in a Christian home," Kinkade remembers. "But I sort of had a rebellious spirit. I didn't have that personal relationship to God in any meaningful way."

After developing a personal relationship to God, Kinkade realized it would change his life. But, like many others, his expectations were not exactly what God had in mind for him.

Kinkade recalls with a bit of a chuckle in his voice that he thought, "Now that I'm a Christian, I should go serve the Lord in something that's really going to be painful to do. A major sacrifice. Maybe I'll become a missionary to a third-world country."

He continues softly, "I remember the sweet way the Lord began to give me revelation. Do I have any knowledge of Africa? No. Do I have any special preparation to go to Africa? No. Do I have the money to go to Africa? No. Do I speak any language spoken there? No. I didn't in any way fit in or have any reason that that would be a logical and effective use of this prepackaging the Lord had done in my life. I have all this experience, divinely appointed, that led me into this particular talent or gift— whatever you would call it—in painting, drawing, fine art, and here I wanted to throw all that away! What an inefficient thing!

"I discovered that I could use my talent to serve the Lord. I committed it to Him and immediately began to make my living. I always say, when I got saved, my art got saved," Kinkade concludes.

As part of his newly rediscovered faith, Kinkade began studying the Scriptures and found that "light," a word that had long been applied to his paintings, was also a key word in describing God. "Light is the characteristic more than any other that defines God. His own self-description is light," Kinkade states. "I didn't know that. It's something God revealed to me."

His favorite verse, Matthew 5:16, "Let your light so shine before men, that they see your good works, and glorify your Father which is in heaven," came to Kinkade not like a bolt out of the blue, but more like the feeling of completeness you get the moment you place a perfect ornament on top of a wonderful Christmas tree.

"There was a period of a year or more where I had intense word study every morning," Kinkade recalls. Down in the barn that was his studio, he found himself reflecting on biblical references to light like "Christ is the Light of the world, and Thy word is a light unto my feet," and others that showed how pervasive God's light is.

"I began to see more and more that God intended me to focus my ministry on letting my light shine. By letting my light shine (though my work), God's light can simply shine out through my paintings," Kinkade emphasizes. This soul-deep connection between the Bible verse and the realization that he is called to let his light "so shine before men" led him to know that this particular verse talks to him very personally.

While Kinkade speaks reverently about his connection to this verse, he sees some humor in the situation, too. "It dawned on me that God had a particular purpose for my life, which I still find incredibly hilarious, because I live with myself every day and there's nothing special about me. There's no reason why God would have chosen me, except for the fact he knew I'm available. Nothing else."

Finally, Kinkade admits that having given his talents to

his ministry for God has sometimes put him in an unusual position for an artist. "You know, in any given month, I get hundreds of letters from people all over the country. It's a funny thing, when they write me, rarely do they comment on anything I can take credit for. I mean, I rarely hear comments about my use of brushwork, my use of color, my ability to create mood, my technique, or my composition, although I wish they would many times. It would be very satisfying if they said, 'I had to write you to tell you that you were really able to capture the effect of autumn foliage in that latest painting.' But they don't write to say that. They write to say, 'Something in that painting touched me and changed my life. Touched my heart. I saw the depth of God's grace, His love, in that painting.' "

Kinkade adds modestly, "I've seen that testimony so many times at this point that I've got to feel that God, in spite of me, has chosen somehow to use these paintings. I give Him total credit for it."

Judging
Each Other

St. Matthew 7:1-2

Judge not, that ye be not judged. For with what judgment ye judge, ye shall be judged: and with what measure ye mete, it shall be measured to you again.

Fred Rogers

A warm, modest, and scholarly man, Fred responds to a question about what he would like to see in his introduction by immediately mentioning his pleasure at being a husband, the father of two sons, and the grandfather of two boys. Many other people might have started by stating that they were the host of Mister Rogers' Neighborhood, *the longest-running children's program on public television, the recipient of two Peabody Awards and an Emmy for Lifetime Achievement, as well as honorary degrees from over thirty-two colleges and universities. But not him. Today, Fred lovingly continues to create new episodes for* Mister Rogers' Neighborhood, *writes books and music, and makes the world a better place for children of all ages.*

Picking a single Scripture to talk about was incredibly difficult for Fred. He has so many favorites, especially about love and children (in fact, he was very pleased that Bil Keane had taken St. Matthew 19:13–14). Yet, after some consideration, he chose Bible verses that talk about judging.

"Some may think its very unlike me to choose Scripture

that talks about judgment," states Fred. "And yet, I think that it's so important, that if somebody else doesn't choose it, I really should, because I'm terribly concerned about the judgmental attitude of a lot of our society."

He deplores what he calls "the pointing of fingers and the not being able to put oneself in somebody else's shoes. I think that's what Jesus did. I think he constantly put Himself in other people's shoes, just like the Indian saying, 'You don't judge anybody until you've walked a mile in their moccasins.' "

While musing about the nature of judgment and how our judging other people affects us, Fred mentions, "I wonder if in this verse that we're talking about, there's some eternal wrapping (binding us together). I'm not being morbid about it, I'm just talking about death being one of the great levelers in human life. Even kings die."

He says that the Hebrew word "satan" literally means "accuser," and he sees that as the very opposite of what Jesus is, and that the Holy Spirit was promised as a spirit of advocacy. He envisions a judgment day when "the accuser will do all he or she can to convince the Eternal that we are not acceptable while the spirit of the advocate, unconditional love, will do all that he or she can to help convince the final judge that we truly deserve eternal grace."

On an everyday level, Fred notes that having a judgmental attitude is not only very damaging, it can keep people from recognizing wonderful gifts and opportunities. He remembers a time when he was so wrapped up in judging another, he nearly missed the blessing that the event held.

"One time I was in Nantucket," Fred recalls. "I had

heard that there was going to be this famous preacher at the chapel on Sunday. I was still in seminary then, and a student of homiletics (the art of preparing and delivering sermons). I wanted so much to hear this famous preacher. So my wife and I and two friends of ours, Cliff and Dotty, went to this chapel and we discovered that the famous preacher had not been able to come to the island and an eighty-some-year-old minister was filling in for him.

"Well, I was *really* disappointed. I sat there listening to probably one of the worst sermons I've ever heard in my life. I was thinking that, according to homiletics class, this man was going against every rule of good preaching.

"When it was all over, thank goodness I didn't say anything. I looked to my left, and there was Dotty with tears in her eyes. She whispered to me, 'He said exactly what I needed to hear.'

"That was one of the seminal moments in my life. It was one of the greatest lessons. Because what I realized then was that I had come in judgment and she had come in need. Whatever those words were in that sermon of his, the Holy Spirit somehow took them and translated them from his mouth to her ears in a way that was very healing for her."

Along with being careful not to be judgmental of others, Fred recognizes that there are times when people need to let go of judging themselves. Even though he and his staff work very diligently on every program, he says, "I know that there have been times when I thought a program that I had done was far less than I wanted it to be. It seemed to me that just nothing had gone right. Well, I would later get a letter citing that particular program as one of the most helpful things that this viewer had seen or heard. So I realized that all we can do is do our best and hope that it can somehow help somebody else. Realize that doing what you could do at the moment is acceptable by the One who is our Eternal Advocate."

When Fred looks back on "that Sunday" in the chapel, he says, "Thank God that famous minister was not able to come to the island that day!" If he had, he would probably have given a rousing sermon. However, in sitting there, going from judgment to awe at the impact of that "flawed" sermon, Fred learned a lesson that has stayed with him through a lifetime. Judging other people and their efforts is for God, not human beings.

In a way, it is also a lesson that Fred's grandfather, Mr. McFeely, had sought to teach his grandson—the man who is now America's grandfather—when he was a boy. Even though Fred was not physically robust and was somewhat lonely, his grandfather did not judge him negatively. One day he told Fred, "There's only one person in the whole world like you, and I happen to like you just the way you are."

Today, those touching words, spoken by his grandfather many decades ago, reach out to comfort and encourage the children who visit in *Mister Rogers' Neighborhood*. When you watch Fred, you know he completely lets go of any judgment and really means it when he tells them, "I happen to like you, just the way you are."

Jesus Blesses the Children

St. Matthew 19:13-14

Then were there brought unto him (Jesus) little children, that he should put his hands on them, and pray: and the disciples rebuked them.

But Jesus said, Suffer (let) little children, and forbid them not, to come unto me: for of such is the kingdom of heaven.

Bil Keane

Cartoonist Keane is the creator of Family Circus, *the most widely syndicated cartoon panel in America. The recipient of many awards, including the Reuben Award, the highest honor cartoonists can bestow on their peers, Keane is beloved by the public for his cartoons and his efforts to promote reading and self-esteem among children.*

"If there is any one word that can describe what a cartoon should be, that word is 'simple,' " states Keane. "I think this passage of the Bible typifies the word simple . . . the innocence of a small child.

"A number of my cartoons, and the ones that really cause the most comment and draw the most mail, are the ones that have a poignant subject or convey a very tender, loving feeling. That is an emotion I like to nurture in the readers which I consider more important than the belly laugh. I'd rather have the cartoon that will touch their heart or give them a lump in the throat or a tear in the eye."

Family Circus first appeared on February 29, 1960, in only nineteen papers. Over time it has grown steadily as a result of its ability to connect people of all cultures with its touching reflections of family life. Currently, *Family Circus* runs in over fifteen hundred papers worldwide and is read by one hundred million people. Along with three animated holiday specials on NBC, there are over fourteen million Fawcett books in print and a new book, *Count Your Blessings*, has been published by Focus on the Family.

In this Bible story, Jesus is sitting, perhaps on a smooth rock, waiting to welcome the children and share His love without any hidden agenda. Keane also came into cartooning from a desire to share the feelings of love that a family experiences. "It's really a labor of love," he explains. "I never expected it to be as widely syndicated as it has become."

One thing that sets *Family Circus* apart from other panels (single-image cartoons) and strips (a series of related panels) is Keane's willingness to be open about his faith in his work. It wasn't always easy.

"Many years ago when I first began, if I mentioned God in the cartoon, I would get letters of criticism from people out there for putting God's name in a comic," remembers Keane. "They'd say it was almost blasphemous! And yet, today, the same people write to me and say, 'Congratulations on adding a bit of spiritual message or having a Christian slant and voice on the comic page, where it's most needed.' The pendulum has swung to where people are recognizing a deity."

The fact is, according to polls done by the Gallup Organization, 96 percent of America's population believe in God or a universal spirit and 86 percent say that religion is very or fairly important in their lives. So when the *Family Circus* family goes to church, it is an experience that nearly everyone can identify with because of their experiences within their own faith.

Keane has also used the simplicity of message in the story of Jesus blessing the children to help people cope with the emotional burden of missing a loved one who has died.

His own father died four years before Keane started *Family Circus*. In loving memory, he has added his father to the strip as the Granddad who is in heaven. At different times, Granddad has been seen watching his family's antics from a fluffy cloud, standing beside them during difficult times, and even playing catch with Farley, the family pet from Lynn Johnston's *For Better or for Worse* strip, after the aged dog had died saving the youngest daughter's life.

"My dad, when he died, never knew that he would be seen by millions of people. I try to make it not eerie or ghostlike as much as pleasant. To let—especially the kids—know in a graphic way that there is a hereafter. When they put a dead person into a grave or cremate them, it's not the end. There's life after death," Keane says thoughtfully.

But, as in real life, not everyone in heaven died as an adult. In one of his 1991 panels, Keane remembers Jeffy having a thought balloon over his head that showed letting the children come to Jesus just like in the Bible story. At the same time Jeffy is thinking of heaven, Keane had drawn angels and many dozens of different children doing all sorts of fun things. According to Keane, "This was sort of an illustration of how a child would interpret getting into heaven." Again, echoing his favorite Bible story,

Keane continues, "You have a better chance of getting in there if you are like a child."

This thinking like a child has had a profound impact on Keane and his work. "I like the idea of a person thinking as a child and keeping the simplicity of a child's mentality in everything they do all through their lives. I think it is important that you approach things from an innocent standpoint and also have the maturity of a grownup's evaluation. In my estimation, most creative people are still children in their minds and the way they think."

Keane adds about this Bible story, "I really do think the reason that particular Bible passage has a very significant meaning to me is because it is the way I express myself in the cartoon."

The ability to get across a complex message in a simple panel is Keane's special gift. Keane admits, "That is the secret behind doing a successful panel cartoon. It has to be immediate and you eliminate the extraneous things. You don't have to tell readers what happened just before. You don't have to tell them what happens after. It's that frozen moment you put your finger on that triggers an identity for the reader."

Jesus said, "Truly I tell you, whoever does not receive the kingdom of God as a little child will never enter it." Keane has taken that message to heart, and through his *Family Circus* panels, he has helped show millions of people how to see their lives—and their faith—through the eyes and heart of a child.

The Story of the Talents

St. Matthew 25:14-30

For the kingdom of heaven is as a man travelling into a far country, who called his own servants, and delivered unto them his goods. Unto one he gave five talents (a coin worth, at today's value, thousands of dollars), and to another two, and to another one; to every man according to his several ability; and straightway took his journey.

Then he that had received the five talents went and traded with the same, and made them other five talents. Likewise he that had received two, he also gained (an)other two. But he that had received one went and digged in the earth, and hid his lord's money.

After a long time, the lord of those servants cometh, and reckoneth with them. And so he that had received five talents came and brought other five talents, saying, Lord, thou deliveredst unto me five talents: behold, I have gained beside them five talents more. His lord said unto him, Well done, thou good and faithful servant: thou hast been faithful over a few things, I will make thee ruler over many things: enter thou into the joy of thy lord. He also that had received two talents came and said, Lord, thou deliveredst unto me two talents: behold, I have gained two other talents beside them. His lord said unto him, Well done, good and faithful servant; thou hast been faithful over a few things, I will make thee ruler over many things: enter thou into the joy of thy lord. Then he which had received the one talent came and said, Lord, I knew thee that thou art an hard man, reaping where thou hast not sown, and gathering where thou hast not strawed: I was afraid, and went and hid thy talent in the earth: lo, there thou hast that (which) is thine. His lord answered and said unto him, Thou wicked and slothful servant, thou knewest that I reap where I sowed not, and gather where I have not strawed: Thou oughtest therefore to have put my money to the exchangers, and then at my coming I should have received mine own with usury. Take therefore the talent from him, and give it unto him which hath ten talents. For unto every one that hath shall be given, and he shall have abundance: but from him that hath not shall be taken away even that which he hath. Cast ye the unprofitable servant into outer darkness.

Nichelle Nichols

Known worldwide as Lt. Uhura, the role she created on the Star Trek *television program and movies, Nichelle Nichols is a gifted singer, dancer, artist, and writer. She frequently tours with her one-woman musical theater show,* Reflections. *Her latest CD album is titled* Nichelle ... Out of This World, *and her books include the auto-biographical* Beyond Uhura *and the science-fiction novel* Saturn's Child.

Somehow the story of the Talents seems absolutely appropriate for Nichelle Nichols because "talent" is a word that keeps coming up in any discussion about her. She has worked with many of the outstanding stars of several generations, including Duke Ellington, Sidney Poitier, Sammy Davis Jr., Pearl Bailey, Dorothy Dandridge, and, of course, the cast of *Star Trek*.

Whether she is singing a touching ballad or delivering lines as an actress, the use of words and language is critical to what she does. One of the interesting things about language is the way words can have different meanings. For instance, the word "tie" as a noun can be a strip of decorative fabric wrapped around a man's neck, but "tie" as a verb is what he does to that fabric to make a knot in it. The word "talent" in this Bible story refers to a coin that was so valuable that it was worth as much then as several thousand dollars would be now. The same word also refers to a superior and apparently natural ability in the arts or sciences.

According to Nichelle, that is no accident. "The parable, of course, is quite appropriate because it really has that meaning for you. When you are given talents, you must not waste them," Nichelle states emphatically. "Simply don't waste your God-given talents. I think there is something sinful about not using them. I don't mean in that everyday sense of good and evil. I think you sin against yourself."

Sometimes, people waste some of their talents because they are willing to believe that someone else knows more about what they can do than they themselves do. As a young child, Nichelle studied ballet to help strengthen and build her up so she could overcome health problems. By the time she was an adolescent, she'd become passionate about becoming a professional ballerina. Even though the ballet master originally wanted to deny her the chance to try because of her skin color, Nichelle auditioned for, and was accepted by, the Chicago Ballet Academy.

But like most people, she still had a part of her that believed authority figures knew what they were talking about. In high school, the whole direction of her life was changed when a counselor convinced her that there were not—and would not be—any black ballerinas. Nichelle gave up on her dream of being a professional ballerina.

"Within that year," Nichelle recounts quietly, "Carmen deLavallade burst forth on *Time* magazine's cover as the first black ballerina at the Metropolitan Opera. It was stunning because I had changed my life! I had believed the counselor! I had violated my father's good counsel and believed someone else who told me I *couldn't* do something."

When asked if she ever allowed anyone else to convince her that she couldn't do something, she responds emphatically, "Never again. Never *ever* again. It was one of those life-changing experiences. It really affected me. I think that is the most violent effect of racism. I think she really felt she was preparing me for this 'terrible world' I would be facing in my naive expectations. In so doing, she stunted my expectations."

Ironically, Nichelle nearly walked away from the role that made her famous because she thought it was not allowing her to use her talents the way she thought they should be used. Gene Roddenberry cast her as *Star Trek*'s communications officer Lt. Uhura (the name is taken from the Swahili word *uhuru*, which means "freedom"). But, as she recalls, network "suits" were very unhappy at the idea of a smart, black woman playing an officer. They kept her from getting a contract the first year and forced her to work as a day player.

"After the first year, I was going to leave the show," Nichelle remembers. "I remember vividly going to Gene and telling him that I was going to leave, I was not going to stay for the second year, and his being very upset and asking me to take the weekend and think about it. I said I would."

That weekend, a chance encounter showed Nichelle that sometimes even when people think they are not using their talents to their best purposes, God may have a reason for them to be doing that thing which uses those persons to His benefit in ways they had not even imagined.

"I remember that I had gone out—and to this day I still think it was an NAACP (National Association for the Advancement of Colored People) fund-raiser because of the people who were there. Someone came up to me and said charmingly and jokingly, 'There's a fan who wants to meet you.' " Unknown to Nichelle, that person had been talking with Dr. Martin Luther King, who had asked to be introduced to Nichelle because he was a big fan of hers.

"So I turned to this man, thinking it's a fan—someone you don't know who has seen you and enjoys your work—and BOOM! There was Dr. Martin Luther King. I actually was just stunned!"

She was astounded when Dr. King told her that he was definitely the fan. During their conversation, Nichelle told him that she was planning to quit the show. Dr. King told her emphatically that she could not and must not quit.

"Don't you realize how important your presence, your character is?" she quotes Dr. King. "Don't you realize the gift this man (Gene Roddenberry) has given the world?"

The job Nichelle was seeing as undesirable, Dr. King was seeing as a groundbreaking opportunity. The characters on *Star Trek* lived together as equals. She, as Uhura, was the first black person to have a truly nonstereotypical role on television. Uhura was a role model for people of all races, and especially children of color who finally saw a black actress portraying a respected professional.

Nichelle stayed with the show, and recognized and embraced the ability that Uhura gave her to inspire others. By being open to this, she found new opportunities to give inspiration in ways that never would have become possible before.

In 1977, Nichelle was invited to speak at the National Space Institute, where she challenged NASA to include women and minorities as astronauts on future missions. Her timing could not have been better. While the early astronauts had been test pilots, the new space shuttle missions were going to need astronauts with many different skills. However, recruiting efforts had lagged, and only months before the crew was to be chosen, there were no women or minorities who had qualified for the program. NASA officials answered her challenge with one of their own. Would she help recruit?

Jumping to take the challenge, Nichelle created an ambitious program including a media blitz, and set out across the country. In the seven months before she began, NASA had received only 1,600 applications; women and minorities constituted fewer than 100 of them. Over the next few months, that figure soared to 8,400 applications, including 1,649 from women and over 1,000 from minorities. The white-male image of the astronaut corps was forever changed by the qualified women and minorities who applied during this period, including Sally Ride, Fred Gregory, Guy Bluford, Judith Resnik, and Ellison Onizuka.

When asked how she feels about the talents that have enabled her to inspire so many people, Nichelle says, "It's uplifting and humbling at the same time. It's the most gratifying reward that you can possibly receive. Knowing that something you did or said or gave of yourself inspired someone else to do better for themselves."

Bettering herself is something that Nichelle is always

working toward. While being interviewed for this book, she mentioned that on one hand, she pours her energy into the things she loves. "I love doing everything," she notes happily. "So if I'm not acting, I'm singing. If I'm not singing, I'm writing. If I'm not writing, I'm building. I'm doing something."

Yet, at the same time, the story of the Talents reminds her that there is always room for improvement. In her case, she sees that as being especially relevant when it comes to procrastination.

"I'm confessing to you now, one of God's problems with me is I am a procrastinator. So I will put off until tomorrow what I should have done today," she admits reluctantly. "Procrastination is a waste of talent and yet it's something I've lived with . . . and tolerated. It's something I don't think I can tolerate anymore." Chuckling, Nichelle says that she had originally planned to talk about another story that had been very inspirational in her life. Then she decided to go with the story of the Talents even though she felt she had understood it her whole life. Yet, she admits that until now, she had not really thought of procrastination as a way of not using her talents to the fullest in the way this Bible story teaches.

"I originally was going to the first story that came to mind," she states. "But maybe God is saying, 'You don't have to beat a dead horse. You've already learned that one. You're going to go back and learn this one!' Never waste your talents, not even for a day!"

Somewhat surprised by the new insight into a story she already loved and lived by, Nichelle declares that she's rededicating her life now. One project she acknowledges she's been procrastinating on is her second novel featuring her intergalactic heroine Saturna. She says she'll be attacking this project with renewed energy. When Nichelle makes a firm commitment to any aspect of her career, she follows through with all her formidable energy and talent, so that book should be available soon!

Jesus in Gethsemane

St. Matthew 26:36-45

Then cometh Jesus with them unto a place called Gethsemane, and saith unto the disciples, Sit ye here, while I go and pray yonder. He took with him Peter and the two sons of Zebedee, and began to be sorrowful and very heavy. Then saith he unto them, My soul is exceeding sorrowful, even unto death: tarry ye here, and watch with me. He went a little farther, and fell on his face, and prayed, saying, O my Father, if it be possible, let this cup pass from me: nevertheless not as I will, but as thou wilt. He cometh unto the disciples, and findeth them asleep, and saith unto Peter, What, could ye not watch with me one hour? Watch and pray, that ye enter not into temptation: the spirit indeed is willing, but the flesh is weak. He went away again the second time, and prayed, saying, O my Father, if this cup may not pass away from me, except I drink it, thy will be done. He came and found them asleep again: for their eyes were heavy. He left them, and went away again, and prayed the third time, saying the same words.

Then cometh he to his disciples, and saith unto them, Sleep on now, and take your rest: behold, the hour is at hand, and the Son of man is betrayed into the hands of sinners.

Paul Petersen

Growing up as a high-profile performer playing the son, Jeff, on the Donna Reed Show, *Paul undoubtedly knows as much about the lifestyle of young performers as anyone alive. Following the suicide of his peer, Rusty Hamer, he founded and is president of A Minor Consideration, a nonprofit support and assistance foundation to aid current and former child stars. He continues to express his artistic talents through his writing. Paul is the author of sixteen books, including* It's a Wonderful Life Trivia Book *(written with Jimmy Hawkins) and the upcoming* A Minor Consideration.

Sometimes, as in the story of Jesus in Gethsemane, people are given a difficult mission in life. They may not want to do what needs to be done, but they realize that it has to be done—and they are the person who has to do it.

Paul was certainly not thinking about assuming a new mission in life on the fateful morning in 1990. Snuggled down in his bed, he was enjoying a few minutes of listening to the *CBS Morning News* before he had to get up and start his busy day. The mood changed abruptly when the announcer told of the suicide of fellow child star Rusty Hamer, who had played the son on *Make Room for Daddy*.

"The moment I heard," Paul recounts, "I sat bolt upright in bed, and in a flash I was given a task. In that moment, not only was I given the task, I was shown how to do it." His new mission was to protect child actors and other professional children in the arts and athletics so that they could grow up into whole people who would be able to benefit from the work they did as children.

The concept of helping professional children was not completely new. Paul recalls, "I had first written about this subject of young professionals in the book *Walt, Mickey and Me*, in 1977, but I was ineffective in prosecuting my beliefs and getting people to understand because I was angry, I was frustrated, and I couldn't do it.

"On that morning, it seemed, when I called looking for help for the six other kid actors that I knew were in pretty much similar situations to Rusty Hamer's, every person I called took my call and made offers of help. Sincere offers of help. The youngsters who became my first target—people like Jay North, who played Dennis the Menace, people like Danny Bonaducci (*The Partridge Family*), people like Todd Bridges (*Diff'rent Strokes*)—welcomed the help."

Paul found that people were anguished by a series of recent tragedies. Besides Rusty Hamer, Tim Hovey (a film actor whose credits included *The Private War of Major Benton*) and Trents Lehman (*The Nanny and the Professor*) were dead by their own hand. Countless other child actors, many now grown to adulthood, were only making appearances in the newspapers and tabloids that recounted their latest brushes with the law.

Setting out to save lives can be pretty frightening, as Paul soon discovered. "I was scared to death because I was saying I would find things like $50,000 for medical procedures. I was telling people that I would find them counseling. I would pay their rent. All sorts of things. I was making promises that if people hadn't helped me, I couldn't have kept.

"Then, remarkably, a group of former kid stars began to lend their time and talents, and 6 people became 60 people became 160 people, and today there are nearly 500 former kid stars involved in A Minor Consideration."

Even with people willing to help out, Paul knew right from the beginning that A Minor Consideration was going to entail significant personal sacrifices. "I had to sit down and have a conversation with my wife and say that in order to do this, we are frankly going to be impoverished—and at the beginning we were," Paul remembers.

Along with the financial sacrifices came the personal and professional sacrifices that had to be made if A Minor Consideration was going to have a chance to succeed. This is where Paul looks to the story of Jesus in Gethsemane for strength.

"When you are certain in your heart of what you know," he states, "there are often times that you have to carry on alone. It's amazing how no matter how you try to deny it, you end up using words from the Bible, particularly the Lord's Prayer (Matt. 6:9–13) to get you through stuff.

"I feel distressed about the sacrifices that are necessary to continue this advocacy. I didn't ask for this burden, I was given this," Paul admits thoughtfully. "There's not a big line behind me willing to take my place should I falter.

Frankly, as an adult man, I recognize that I have to, in fact, train my replacements because the issues surrounding children are not going to go away."

Along with helping former child stars who have fallen on hard times, Paul and A Minor Consideration are very active in protecting the professional children of today. "The experience of the professional child is so contrary to ordinary childhood, that it sets up a dynamic that can lead to long-term, lifelong consequences. It is done so thoughtlessly by naive and inexperienced parents, who often fall victim to predatory managers, agents, and producers. The need to establish guidelines is what we're about. Sometimes it's as elemental as living up to the promises that Hollywood makes but never keeps.

"For example, most people in the country believe that children who work automatically have money set aside for them. That is untrue—or rather, it is true for only 3 percent of the work that children do." That 3 percent is children who have long-term contracts to perform on episodic television shows or as recording artists, or who have endorsement deals in the sports world. In addition, that 3 percent is only the children whose work is covered by the Coogan Law in California or similar but weaker laws in New York and New Jersey.

"Most people assume that when you had a studio schoolteacher and did your work on the set, it was accepted as regular schoolwork at the normal school. Until January 1, 1998, that was untrue. In fact, the kid who worked in the entertainment business was a truant, because there was no excused absence for work in the entertainment business." (Beginning January 1, 1999, there was finally a meaningful accreditation process to ensure that teachers on the set were competent. This was also a result of A Minor Consideration efforts.)

"Most people assume, when they see babies on TV, that these babies are being protected. Well, in California, producers were hiring eight-week premature babies. Eight-week preemies! They were putting them to work because the law only says that the baby has to be fifteen days old. Well, obviously the legislators meant full-term, full birth-weight. But they didn't put it in the law and Hollywood took advantage. When you see a really tiny baby, he's probably still six weeks short of his due date. Well, we passed AB744 in California last year to eliminate that practice."

Along with legislation, the years of advocacy for professional children is paying off on a one-to-one basis, too. Adult actors and others on the set are now calling Paul when they see a situation where a child is not being treated properly. "When they see something, instead of saying, 'Gee, that's bothering me,' they know who to call. We provide a function that has long been needed, and it's almost laughable to me when I reveal this; we have a formal institution to take care of the welfare of animals in this industry, but none for children."

What kinds of problems cause people to call Paul and A Minor Consideration? He tells of three cases, all involving child actors on major television programs. (Author's note: I am purposely being vague about details to protect the privacy of the children involved.)

In the first instance, an adolescent actor was the victim of verbal and sexual harassment from an adult performer on a prime-time show. A Minor Consideration was able to help the parent remove the child from the program in such a way that a financial settlement was reached to benefit the child.

In the second instance, a major star realized that some children working on his program did not have a positive home situation. Paul was brought in, and through A Minor Consideration, he was able to bring in professional services, including psychologists and financial advisers, to counsel the parents and help stabilize the family situation. Paul notes with justifiable pride, "After four years, the children were not damaged. Their money was protected. The families were not blown apart and the children have gone on to better lives."

There was another case involving a young actor whose family was of modest means until he was cast as a regular in a television show. Only a few weeks after he started, his parent showed up at the studio driving a brand-new luxury car. Paul was called and was on the set within two hours. Within three hours the car was on its way back to the dealership.

"Those are the kinds of things we do," Paul states. "Also, now that we are established and known, when we show up on a set, (people know) we're there for a reason and it gets oh, so quiet.

"I'd love not to be bothered. I'd love to have confidence that the kids are getting their education and their money is protected and all the adults surrounding them are treating them well, but that's not the case. That is routinely not the case.

"But it is a happy circumstance that once we do appear on the scene, people really do fear our access to the media and the fact that we can't be fooled—and they reform. Because to be blunt about it, it doesn't pay to anger us. I will call the Department of Social Services. I will call the police. And I will be on the news that evening. That's one thing that Hollywood fears."

Paul explains that the reason parents can suddenly purchase luxury cars and other expensive items when their child gets a job in the entertainment business is simple. The money the child earns actually belongs to the parent. He explains, "Under federal law, the parents of the working child are entitled to its custody, income and services. In other words, children belong to their parents. They are chattel (property—much like cattle or real estate)."

Fortunately, according to Paul, there are many professional children who have wonderful and positive careers. Many people assume that Paul was one of the child actors who lived a horror story. "Some people assume that I was battered and abused and people stole my money, and that must be why I do what I do, but that's not the truth." The truth is that the unseen tap on the shoulder the morning he learned Rusty Hamer had committed suicide was the motivation that got him started.

Paul readily admits that like him, many child performers have loving and caring parents who are working hard to help their children have a good working experience and put aside their earnings for later. "A mature and responsible adult who is the caregiver of a child in this business can, in fact, make a string of decisions that can make this experience a wonder. It can happen. It's rare, that's the problem.

"It takes a strong moral and spiritual base to resist the temptation to do the easy thing. It's easy for parents, after looking at their kid working a ten-hour day on a series, to say yes to an after-hours interview or a weekend appearance when the kid should be playing stickball with friends. It's too easy to say, 'Yes, we'll fly to Chicago and sign autographs for $5,000,' and it takes character for parents to resist that. It takes character for parents to live within their income and not rely on the money generated by the child."

For now, Paul's personal struggle in Gethsemane continues. He works tirelessly to ensure safe, wholesome working experiences for professional children so they can grow into healthy, happy adults who are able to benefit from their youthful professional work. At the same time, he is building an organization that will outlive him so that future generations of professional children will be protected.

Through A Minor Consideration, Paul is able to right wrongs on an individual and industry wide level. The satisfactions are many, but the burden is always there. He concludes thoughtfully, "I think that in the end, a life is worthwhile if it is lived for a cause larger than itself. It's OK to live for other people, and in fact the world is a better place when we do."

You can learn more about A Minor Consideration by visiting their web site at http://www.minorcon.org.

Jesus Heals
the Leper

St. Luke 5:12-14

And it came to pass, when he (Jesus) was in a certain city, behold a man full of leprosy: who seeing Jesus fell on his face, and besought (begged a favor of) him, saying, Lord, if thou wilt, thou canst make me clean. He put forth his hand, and touched him, saying, I will: be thou clean. Immediately the leprosy departed from him. And he (Jesus) charged him to tell no man: but go, and shew (show) thyself to the priest, and offer for thy cleansing, according as Moses commanded, for a testimony unto them.

George Gallup, Jr.

Primarily known for his work in developing authoritative and dependable information on opinions and trends, George Gallup, Jr., is chairman of the George H. Gallup International Institute and cochair of the Gallup Organization. At the same time, he is a thoughtful analyst of how the information his organizations gather can be used to improve life for all people. Gallup is the author, with Timothy Jones, of The Saints Among Us.

To many people, this story of healing a leper is so brief and low-key that they can skim right over it without even noticing it. But when George Gallup, Jr., reads it, it comes to life as a challenge not only for him personally, but for society as a whole.

"This story speaks powerfully to the very heart of Christianity—the requirement to show love to *everyone*—and is, I believe a message to the church today," Gallup states unequivocally. "To encourage people to reach out to the margins of society, to go beyond our comfort zones and embrace those who are 'unlovable'—the murderers, the child abusers, persons with horrible diseases, the dirty and unkempt. To embrace them and show them love."

This urge to recognize and help people who otherwise might be voiceless and ignored in society is not something new in his life. Gallup grew up in a family where giving a voice to the voiceless was more than an idea, it was a motivating factor in the creation of the family business— the Gallup Organization.

Opinion surveys in newspapers date back to the 1820s and have always been a popular item. Over time, they led to market research, but there were problems with accuracy. Lists of potential interviewees were taken from sources such as magazine subscription lists and automobile registration records. Realizing that this left whole segments voiceless and skewed the results, George Gallup, Jr.'s, father, George Gallup, developed a quota-sampling method that enabled all segments of society to be heard and acknowledged in surveys he did. The amazingly accurate results changed the opinion survey industry permanently, and for the better. Growing up, George, Jr., learned how important each voice is in our society. Even today, he is working on a project to try to reach inner-city youth because this is one group of people who are missed in almost all surveys. Gallup says that this 3 or 4 percent is hard to reach because they are transient.

If being a transient makes you voiceless today, in Jesus' time being a leper made you the most voiceless person in the world. Gallup notes that back then, people would even try to avoid being down wind of a leper for fear that they might catch this dreaded disease. To all intents and purposes, lepers were considered to be the walking dead. Yet when the leper came up to Him and begged to be healed, Jesus immediately reached out and touched him.

That the leper would have a faith so strong that it gave

him the audacity to overcome his society's rules against lepers approaching people is quite amazing to Gallup. When asked how the leper's faith impacted this story, he responds, "Tremendously! He went up to Jesus with confidence which is thrilling. He also went with expectancy, humility, and that's so true of all the miracles. It's the heart of the receiver that is the key. The absolute faith."

Then, just as the depth of faith the leper must have felt begins to register on the reader, the story takes another amazing turn. "I just think that Jesus did the unthinkable," Gallup says with amazement. "People just didn't get near lepers! But to me it (reaching out to the leper) was just a stunning example of who Jesus is and what he's all about.

"In a way, it's almost the most spectacular miracle, even though it's not flashy," Gallup continues. Unlike many famous and spectacular miracles, such as Moses parting the Red Sea and Daniel's survival in the lion's den, this miracle was quiet and personal. Jesus simply reached out, touched the leper, and said, "Be thou clean."

Then Jesus said another remarkable thing. He told the leper to tell no one—just go to show himself to the priest and give the sacrifice of thanksgiving that had been a part of society since Moses' time. Gallup sees this as a natural element of this low-key miracle. Jesus wanted people to come to faith in God because of His message, not the flashy miracles He could perform.

Obviously, this miraculous healing did not remain a secret between Jesus and the leper. It was recorded by Jesus' disciples, who must have witnessed it (it also appears in St. Matthew 8:1–4), and it is likely that a lot of people, including the priests, asked the leper how he came to be cured. Yet this remains one of those small, private miracles that people are able to relate to. A reminder that when a person is feeling unlovable, unhealthy, and unfit for society, Jesus can reach out and, through faith, make them whole.

Gallup adds, "I just think that Jesus did the unthinkable. People just didn't get near lepers. To me, it was just a stunning example of what he's all about. Undoubtedly, he reached incredible numbers of people despite his saying, 'Don't tell anybody.' I think that would be *totally* convicting to a lot of people. That settles it for me, anyway!"

The Prodigal Son

St. Luke 15:11-32

Jesus said, A certain man had two sons: the younger of them said to his father, Father, give me the portion of goods that falleth to me. And he divided unto them his living (the father divided his estate and gave the youngest his inheritance).

Not many days after the younger son gathered all together, and took his journey into a far country, and there wasted his substance with riotous living. When he had spent all, there arose a mighty famine in that land; and he began to be in want.

He went and joined himself to a citizen of that country; and he sent him into his fields to feed swine. He would fain (gladly) have filled his belly with the husks that the swine did eat: and no man gave unto him. When he came to himself, he said, How many hired servants of my father's have bread enough and to spare, and I perish with hunger!

I will arise and go to my father, and will say unto him, Father, I have sinned against heaven, and before thee, and am no more worthy to be called thy son: make me as one of thy hired servants.

He arose, and came to his father. When he was yet a great way off, his father saw him, and had compassion, and ran, and fell on his neck, and kissed him.

The son said unto him, Father, I have sinned against heaven, and in thy sight, and am no more worthy to be called thy son. But the father said to his servants, Bring forth the best robe, and put it on him; and put a ring on his hand, and shoes on his feet: bring hither (here) the fatted calf, and kill it; and let us eat, and be merry: for this my son was dead, and is alive again; he was lost, and is found. They began to be merry.

Now his elder son was in the field: and as he came and drew nigh to the house, he heard musick and dancing. He called one of the servants, and asked what these things meant. He (the servant) said unto him, Thy brother is come; and thy father hath killed the fatted calf, because he hath received him safe and sound.

And he (the elder son) was angry, and would not go in: therefore came his father out, and intreated him (pleaded with him). He (the son) answering said to his father, Lo, these many years do I serve thee, neither transgressed I at any time thy commandment: and yet thou never gavest me a kid, that I might make merry with my friends: but as soon as this thy son was come, which hath devoured thy living with harlots, thou has killed for him the fatted calf.

And he (his father) said to him, Son, thou are ever with me, and all that I have is thine. It was meet (right) that we should make merry, and be glad: for this thy brother was dead, and is alive again; and was lost, and is found.

Joan Wester Anderson

❧

The best-selling author of Where Angels Walk, *which was on the* New York Times Best-Seller List *for over a year, Joan has written a dozen other books. Her latest,* The Power of Miracles, *was published in the fall of 1998. Joan has appeared on many prestigious national television programs and in documentaries including* Angels—Beyond the Light *and* Angel Stories. *She is currently a story consultant for the Pax Network television series* It's a Miracle.

Not every favorite Bible story is love at first sight. Joan admits, "I was always uncomfortable with the parable of the Prodigal Son. I never liked it."

Like many people who are the oldest child in their birth family, Joan identified with the older brother in the story. She, too, had worked hard all her life, trying to do what was right and please those she was responsible to. Then, when she read the older son's plea to his father, she really identified with how betrayed this son must have felt. None of his hard work was ever celebrated. No one had thrown him a party for all the years he had labored to serve his father. Yet here was his brother, a man who had tormented his father with his insistence on taking his inheritance and squandering it on a destructive lifestyle, and their father was throwing him a first-class party.

"This did not fit with the loving Lord that I knew. It seemed to me that there should be some retribution for this guy," Joan says.

"Then, in my thirties and going into my forties, I began to get rather despondent about my writing career. Nothing much was doing, and at the same time, I began to feel this longing to get closer to God." Joan talked with a friend who described the joyful experiences she had at her Charismatic Renewal prayer meetings. Joan admits, "I didn't want to go near them. I thought they were a little strange. Yet I've been a member now for twelve years, so I guess we're all strange. But at the time, it was too much for me. It seemed too emotional."

Thinking about her personal needs, she realized that she really wanted to study the Old Testament. She joined a Scripture study class at her church. "There are times in your faith when you kind of coast, and then there are times when you have to take a step. This was one of those times."

In a very real way, Joan was using the class to help her explore where she wanted to go with her life. She had been writing family humor and self-help books and articles for years, but they were no longer giving her the gratification they once had.

Now, several best-sellers later, when she looks back on that time, Joan says, "So often I've heard people say that the mountaintop experiences in life are wonderful, but nothing grows on top of a mountain—it's only in the valleys that you learn and you grow, because that is where all the activity is. I was in a valley. When you're in a valley, you look up because there is no other direction to look." Looking up to God by taking this class was helping strengthen her for the challenges that lay ahead. It also was helping her learn more about how she fit into God's plans.

The day Joan had the epiphany (flash of insight) that clarified the Prodigal Son for her started like any other in her Scripture class. "I think it was probably the first time I had heard anyone else discuss this parable. There were several oldest children in the room, and we all had the same thing to say—we had always hated it so much. So our Bible teacher started asking us to go over the parable one line at a time. When we got to a certain line, it was like the sun had broken through for all of us, because the line was when the father was talking to the older son, who was complaining bitterly that he never got a party. The father says something that I had always overlooked. He said, 'My son, you have always been my son and everything I have is yours. But we have to celebrate because the lost child has come home.'

"I saw for the first time that I had always thought that love was limited. That if someone else got some of it, then that would mean that mine was diminished in some way. But here was this father saying to the son that he had enough love to go around for everybody. That everything he had belonged to the son—and that was true—that the son was going to get the whole inheritance.

"I saw in my mind this vision of how I had once explained love to my children when the fourth baby had been born and my other boys were five, four, and two and a half. While they were somewhat interested in the baby,

I could see they weren't as thrilled as I had hoped. I figured out they might be jealous. One night after dinner, I put a candle in front of each of the boys and another one in the center of the table. I lit the one in the center of the table and said to them, 'This is Mommy's love burning for all of you,' and then I had each of them light the candle in front of them and I said, 'See, the light is still there, but the room is getting brighter.' Then we lit the last candle for the baby, and I showed them that I would have plenty of love for the baby, too." She was showing them, in a way they could understand, that just as the new candle-light for the baby added brightness to the room, so her love for the new baby would increase the love in their home, and not diminish the love she had for them at all.

"When I saw 'Everything I have is yours,' I realized that nothing was lost at all. The oldest brother wouldn't lose a thing by having his brother come back. In fact, his life would probably be helped. Someone would help him on the farm and with all the rest of it. Then I saw how I had limited God so much. I had put such a box around Him, saying, 'I'll go this far but no farther. I'll trust you this much, but no more.' It was the most amazing moment when I saw all of a sudden, through this parable, that everything that the Lord had, had always been mine. I had chosen to accept it early. I had never rebelled, and what a wonderful life I had had because of it. Here was the younger son who had thrown it all away. Probably had a horrible life, living with the pigs, and missing his family."

Joan feels that "No one who leads a sinful life is ever really happy for any length of time. There's always those miserable times that intrude, and I had missed most of that. I had chosen to live my life my Father's way, and I had eliminated so much suffering. So everything that He had ever had was mine, and always had been. From that point on, I thought, there just won't be any more limits. So I did go to the Renewal. I ended up joining the prayer group, and it's been a real mainstay for me."

In addition to taking the leap of faith that led her to join the prayer group, another way Joan broke outside her old limits was by writing about the time an angel saved her son Tim's life in a raging blizzard. Then she found herself sharing the story when she was giving speeches. As she shared her story, people came up to her and told their own personal stories of angelic assistance.

In a casual conversation with a magazine editor she had worked with, Joan mentioned how these stories seemed to be coming together as a book. Unknown to her, this editor and her partner were looking for just the right book to start their own publishing house. A few weeks later, Joan answered the phone and her editor offered to publish the book, which became *Where Angels Walk*.

"I thought it was the last book I would ever do, and it ended up being the first book of a whole new world," Joan says with wonder in her voice.

Since then she has written *An Angel to Watch over Me*, *Where Miracles Happen*, and *Where Wonders Prevail*. She has sold millions of books and had marvelous opportunities that would never have happened when she was still putting limits on God's love and her trust in it.

To learn more about Joan and her work, visit her web site at http://www.mcs.net/~angelwak/home.html

Zaccheus the Tax Collector

St. Luke 19:1-10

Jesus entered and passed through Jericho. Behold, there was a man named Zaccheus, which was the chief among the publicans (tax collectors), and he was rich. He sought to see Jesus who he was; and could not for the press (crowd), because he was little of stature. He ran before, and climbed up into a sycomore tree to see him: for he (Jesus) was to pass that way.

When Jesus came to the place, he looked up, and saw him, and said unto him, Zaccheus, make haste, and come down; for to day I must abide at thy house. And he made haste, and came down, and received him joyfully.

When they saw it, they all murmured, saying, that he (Jesus) was gone to be guest with a man that is a sinner. Zaccheus stood, and said unto the Lord; Behold, Lord, the half of my goods I give to the poor; and if I have taken any thing from any man by false accusation, I restore him fourfold.

Jesus said unto him, This day is salvation come to this house, forsomuch as he also is a son of Abraham. For the Son of man is come to seek and to save that which was lost.

Jeff Smith

Jeff Smith is well known as television's Frugal Gourmet and for his nine cookbooks, including The Frugal Gourmet Keeps the Feast. *He describes himself as a clergyman, a serious child of the church. And "I cook like crazy!"*

"The question is ludicrous!" Smith emphatically proclaims when asked to name his favorite Bible story. "It is as wild as asking me which is my favorite son! I really can't answer that! However, the one that immediately jumped to mind is the story of Zacchaeus."

Too often, Smith believes, the real story of Zacchaeus has been lost behind the few sentences that speak of a man who seems to magically "get religion" (as we might say today) when he's invited to get down out of a tree and fix lunch for Jesus. "This story should knock us off our pews!" Smith exclaims.

To Smith, this is really a story about a man who is so low and vile that he has sold out his people to the Romans in order to gain personal wealth. It is a story about Jesus flagrantly and willfully violating biblical law as it had been understood for countless generations. Only then is it a story about redemption.

The connection between food and the Bible has long fascinated Smith. Many of his books, including, *The Frugal Gourmet Keeps the Feast* and *The Frugal Gourmet Celebrates Christmas,* focus on how food functions as theological talk in the Bible.

One critical fact that was commonly understood back then was that it was against biblical law to be seen eating with an enemy. At the same time, the biblical law of hospitality said that you had to feed the enemy if he was hungry. Of course, this enemy would have to eat off by himself and not with the family, but you still had to feed him. Smith adds, "Because of this, the table became the symbol of intimate communication. The rug that was the table was more intimate than sex."

Zacchaeus was a Jew who had become a tax collector for the Romans. What that meant to the people in his community was that he was making a comfortable living by collecting taxes from them to pay for the Roman soldiers who kept them in captivity. Even his name had the qualities of an ironic curse. Zacchaeus actually means "pure" in Hebrew, but there was nothing pure about the way Zacchaeus led his life.

"Zacchaeus was not a popular boy," Smith recounts. "You cannot imagine anyone lower on the social ladder than Zacchaeus. Although he could eat lamb stew at night when you or I had gruel—because he made so much money off his racket—he had no place in the community except as an enemy. People absolutely hated him!"

Smith continues, "Jesus was raised as a good Jew; we know he had rabbinic training. So we know that he knew the law. He cannot be seen eating with his enemies. Now this is the part of the story we don't talk about in the church. Everyone knows that one is not to be seen eating with the enemy. At the same time, Jesus is preaching about the coming of the kingdom when there can be no enemies. Then Jesus eats with all the wrong people (sinners, enemies, etc.) to make his point. Of course, during this, Jesus looks up into the tree and sees Zacchaeus hanging on with his skinny arms—and there's nothing I've ever found in any biblical text that would give us any indications as to why Jesus could possibly have known this Zacchaeus—and Jesus said, 'I'll be done here in about fifteen minutes. You go home and prepare lunch, and I'll join you shortly.'

"Everyone in the crowd must have gone, 'Ooooh boy, he's gone too far this time.' And sure enough, Jesus went over and had lunch with Zacchaeus. Mystified everyone."

In reality, Jesus was demonstrating a long biblical tradition. For example, in Isaiah 55:1–5 it says that the day will come when we will all eat at one table. The meaning is clearly that there will come a day when there are no enemies and none of the hate and dissension that occur between people when they consider each other to be enemies.

Smith remembers, "I first learned about the table as the place where enemies could not be present when I was in graduate school in 1963–1964, from an old Scottish Presbyterian, John Patterson. Oh, what a lovely man!" Patterson taught that the value of the person in the desert cultures is absolute because he is a member of the tribe, a member of the family, and a member of the household of God. In this context, there can be no enemies because all people are of the family of God.

Does that mean everyone should believe they have no enemies? No. Smith admits to having an "enemies list" of five people. Not the same five people all the time, of course. He challenges everyone to recognize that there are people in their life that they may actively feel are operating in a way that would classify them as enemies.

At the same time, he says, "The biblical image is that eventually we'll all be at the same table and the Messiah will pour the wine and pronounce the presence of the Kingdom and we'll look up and here are those five people, sitting right across from us. That's the most horrifying concept, and I'm going to have to look at those people. I don't understand it—but I must accept it."

So what does Smith think happened to Zacchaeus after the events in the Bible story had unfolded? With a chuckle in his voice, he recounts that in the book of Isaiah, everyone is invited to the feast that encompasses all people. "And there's a guy at the door selling tickets," Smith says conspiratorially. "And good Lord have mercy, it scares people to death. 'Come and buy a ticket. Come and buy without money. Come and buy wine and bread and milk and honey without price,' says the ticket seller.

"So Isaiah is a practical joker. He sets us up for this feast, and when we get there, there is a ticket seller and he gives the tickets out free—and we've been taught there is nothing free in the world, you have to work—work, for the night is coming—and here's this guy passing out tickets. If indeed Zacchaeus was saved, and the texts seem to claim that he was, then he's got to be the guy with the tickets. He's giving them away!"

So the story of Zacchaeus comes down to more than a tale about getting lunch on a hot, dusty day. Smith sees it as a dramatic example of Jesus showing people how their understanding of the Law of God was changing because of his coming. In Matthew 5:17, Jesus says, "Do not think that I have come to abolish the law . . . I come not to abolish but to fulfill [NSRV edition]." In the story of Zacchaeus, Jesus showed us how we must accept our enemies, and that is a profound, life-changing lesson worthy of a fresh look in our lives today.

Water to Wine

St. John 2:1-12

And the third day there was a marriage in Cana of Galilee; and the mother of Jesus was there: Both Jesus was called, and his disciples, to the marriage. When they wanted wine, the mother of Jesus saith unto him, They have no wine. Jesus saith unto her, Woman, what have I to do with thee? mine hour is not yet come. His mother saith unto the servants, Whatsoever he saith unto you, do it. There were set there six waterpots of stone, after the manner of the purifying of the Jews, containing two or three firkins (a firkin is approximately nine gallons) apiece. Jesus saith unto them, Fill the waterpots with water. They filled them up to the brim.

He saith unto them, Draw out now, and bear unto the governor of the feast. And they bare it. When the ruler of the feast had tasted the water that was made wine, and knew not whence it was: (but the servants which drew the water knew;) the governor of the feast called the bridegroom, and saith unto him, Every man at the beginning doth set forth good wine; and when men have well drunk, then that which is worse: but thou hast kept the good wine until now.

This beginning of miracles did Jesus in Cana of Galilee, and manifested forth his glory; and his disciples believed on him.

After this he went down to Capernaum, he, and his mother, and his brethren, and his disciples: and they continued there not many days.

Ruth Stafford Peale

Even in her nineties, when most people have long retired, Ruth Stafford Peale maintains an active and remarkable career. She is chairman of Guideposts (which includes Guideposts magazine, the spiritually inspirational magazine with the largest circulation, and the Peale Center for Christian Living). She and her late, beloved husband, Dr. Norman Vincent Peale, founded Guideposts in 1945. As part of her responsibilities as chairman, Ruth travels widely to promote Guideposts' work and message.

When asked what she thought was so special about this simple Bible story that recounted Jesus' first miracle of turning water into wine at a wedding feast, Ruth says thoughtfully, "I always felt that this was a story that showed the human part of Jesus. That he, first of all, would be invited to a wedding. Then that he was having a good time. He saw that there was a problem, so he solved it by turning the water into wine."

A critical part of the story occurred as Jesus' mother noticed that the host was disturbed when the wine ran out early. So Mary went and told her son about the situation. Even though Jesus had planned just to be part of the party, he quietly had the servants pour water into large pots and he spontaneously turned it into fine wine.

"I think it makes Jesus very human. Down-to-earth," Ruth says persuasively. "Jesus could see that the hostess was very much disturbed by this and he solved the problem for her."

Ruth mentions that when people study the life of Jesus, they often focus on the difficult times He experienced. They study His deep thought. They marvel at His commitment to His mission. They can end up studying Jesus as the Son of God and miss Jesus the man entirely.

"I hope that people understand that Jesus was so human that He wanted people to have fun and relationships in their lives," Ruth concludes. "It was not all work, and it was not all fun, but Jesus was aware that all relationships have meaning in life."

Forgiving the Woman Adulterer

St. John 8:1-11

Jesus went unto the mount of Olives. Early in the morning he came again into the temple, and all the people came unto him; and he sat down, and taught them. The scribes and Pharisees (members of a strictly observant Jewish sect) brought unto him a woman taken in adultery; and when they had set her in the midst, they say unto him, Master, this woman was taken in adultery, in the very act. Now Moses in the law commanded us, that such should be stoned: but what sayest thou? This they said, tempting him, that they might have (cause) to accuse him (of breaking the law). But Jesus stooped down, and with his finger wrote on the ground, as though he heard them not. So when they continued asking him, he lifted up himself, and said unto them, He that is without sin among you, let him first cast a stone at her. Again he stooped down, and wrote on the ground. They which heard it, being convicted by their own conscience, went out one by one, beginning at the eldest, even unto the last: and Jesus was left alone, and the woman standing in the midst. When Jesus had lifted up himself, and saw none but the woman, he said unto her, Woman, where are those thine accusers? hath no man condemned thee? She said, No man, Lord. Jesus said unto her, Neither do I condemn thee: go, and sin no more.

Richard N. Bolles

With over six million copies in print over the last twenty-eight years, Bolles's annually updated book, What Color Is Your Parachute? *is the resource that helps people find the best work for them. His other books include* The Three Boxes of Life, and How to Get Out of Them; Where Do I Go from Here with My Life?; How to Find Your Mission in Life; Job-Hunting Tips for the (So-called) Handicapped; *and* Job-Hunting on the Internet. *Dick is a sought-after speaker and master teacher.*

Like many people in this book, Dick found the idea of picking *only* one Bible story or verse to be quite a challenge. "It's so hard to say, 'Well, this is my favorite moment in the revelation of God to us as to who He is, because I can point to so many great passages," Dick states.

"It's impossible to pick out one story. So what I asked myself is what story do I treasure, particularly in the time in which I find myself living? The story that means the most to me in view of current history is the Gospel according to John, chapter 8:1–11." Along with the story's current importance, it also illuminates a decision Dick faced during a personal tragedy a number of years ago.

In this Bible story, the scribes and Pharisees have caught a woman in the act of adultery. They bring her to Jesus, asking what they should do with her.

"The reason I like this story particularly is twofold. First of all it is, in a sense, a summation of what our whole charter is with God. At the end of it, in the eleventh verse, Jesus asks her if anyone condemned her, and she says, 'No man, Lord,' and he says, 'Neither do I condemn you.' That seems to me to be the verse we need to hear ringing in our ears throughout our lives about our relationship with God. It's all based on forgiveness, not merit.

"Of course, I'm hardly the first person to have discovered this. But it is the essence of the Gospel, the good news that God gives to us about His relationship with us. There isn't anything we can do that can break that relationship. We live in this world where there are so many conditions for maintaining relationships, and we say, 'Well, I'm not going to put up with that!' It's awfully hard for us to get into our thick skulls that God really doesn't treat us the way we treat other people."

Dick's second reason for choosing this story focuses on forgiveness in human relationships. He says, "I think we live in an age that has absolutely lost any understanding of what forgiveness is. We live in an age that thinks that if you can find enough excuses for why somebody did something, then we can 'write off' the deed; and that's the equal of forgiveness. We've taken the idea of 'mitigating circumstances' and utterly substituted it for forgiveness."

Dick sees two distinct characteristics of true forgiveness.

"The first thing is (recognizing) that the thing that was done was utterly, utterly wrong and there is no mitigating circumstance whatsoever. That's the first principle of forgiveness: calling a thing what it is. The second principle is that nonetheless, God forgives this act. That is awesome, because we show how puny our capacity to forgive is by saying, 'I can only forgive this person for this awful, awful deed if I can find some mitigating circumstances or reason that makes it not so awful.' "

For Dick, all of this is not a facile matter. He himself has had to wrestle with the concept of true forgiveness in the midst of a family tragedy. Dick's brother Don Bolles was a nationally known investigative reporter for the *Arizona Republic* newspaper. In 1976, he was brutally assassinated one morning while pursuing a story on local corruption.

On that fateful day, after Don had been lured to a fake meeting, he returned to his Datsun. As he began backing out of his parking place, six sticks of dynamite that had been placed under the driver's seat by John (Harvey) Adamson exploded. Don died eleven agonizing days later, after surgeons had been forced to amputate both legs and one of his arms in a futile attempt to save his life.

This is the kind of tragedy that can embitter people who loved the victim. Dick had a choice to make. Could he forgive the bomber? Or would he let his anger be in control?

When he talks about forgiving, Dick calls it "hard work." He says, "The hard work is saying the sin is terrible, but I still love the sinner. We don't value that hard work, in our culture. In fact, if somebody kills a child and the mother says, 'I've turned to God and I've found forgiveness for this person,' we tend to think she's nuts. I mean, that's the way the culture reads it. 'Come on, lady, get a grip! This is an awful person.' "

While people are attempting the hard work of distinguishing between the sin and the sinner, there is another factor to consider. What is going on inside the forgiver?

"When we look at our lives and see the places where we weren't able to forgive, we know that our inability to forgive is like the corrosive acid in a battery. It eats away at the soul," says Dick. "That's why it's so important for us as individuals, as humans, to forgive, (because of) what it does to us if we don't forgive."

Knowing all this, Dick knew what he had to do about his brother's assassination. "When they (Adamson and his accomplices) were convicted, I was contacted by reporters from everywhere. They called me, and said, 'Well how do you feel now that justice has been done?' The question was whether the malefactors should be executed, particularly John Adamson, who placed the actual bomb.

"I called my mother up and I said to her, 'Mom, I was interviewed by reporters today. I didn't have time to check with you, so I said something you're probably going to disagree with. I said I really don't think they should be executed.' I added, 'I don't think an eye for an eye and a tooth for a tooth is the appropriate response to this.' She said, 'I was interviewed by reporters, too, and I told them the same thing.' "

Some people think that it is impossible to forgive unless the person who did the deed expresses remorse. Dick responds, "The point of forgiveness is what it does for you if you don't." He adds, "The forgiveness isn't done for the sake of the person (who committed the offense), in which case maybe remorse would be required because you're saying, 'We're extending to him a wonderful gift and he has to be ready to receive it or we can't offer it.' But the point of forgiveness is that you offer it anyway. What the person does with it is his business, but you offer the forgiveness nonetheless, even as God does to us."

Dick cautions that forgiving is not just a feel-good exercise. The profound purpose of forgiving is not just to relieve emotional pain; it is to enable people to relate more closely to God. When asked how he feels about people who try to talk about spirituality without any mention of God, he says, "I have a great deal of contempt for that view of spirituality, I'm afraid. It's people trying to milk concepts that have guided us for centuries: forgiveness and spirituality only make sense when rooted in God. These are concepts that have been around for a long, long time in the affairs of humans.

"Our age is the age of idiocy because we act as though we are discovering, for the first time in history, the real truth. We say all those people who lived before us sure missed the boat. They didn't understand these things, but we do. What nonsense! There's no such thing as spirituality that doesn't point to God. That's the whole meaning of it all. Vocation means 'calling.' Someone calls! Enthusiasm means 'God in us.' We attempt to strip down historic words that have meant one central thing down through all the ages and remove God from their center. Then we claim that this is what people should have always believed."

Forgiveness is also a word that has come down through the ages filled with deep meaning. As Dick says, it takes a great deal of work to be able to forgive someone who has sinned against us personally or against our society.

"We have to understand that forgiveness is a part of the relationship we have both with God and with each other. That doesn't mean that we give our unwavering stamp of approval to everything somebody does. Judgment still holds sway. But we can learn to forgive. So I find my mind turning to this story of Jesus and the woman caught in adultery again and again—reflecting on the fact that people don't want to do the hard work of forgiveness in human relationships. But we must learn."

Healing the Blind Man

St. John 9:1-11

As Jesus passed by, he saw a man which was blind from his birth. His disciples asked him, saying, Master, who did sin, this man, or his parents, that he was born blind? Jesus answered, Neither hath this man sinned, nor his parents: but that the works of God should be made manifest in him. I must work the works of him that sent me, while it is day: the night cometh, when no man can work. As long as I am in the world, I am the light of the world. When he had thus spoken, he spat on the ground, and made clay of the spittle, and he anointed the eyes of the blind man with the clay, and said unto him, Go, wash in the pool of Siloam (which is by interpretation, Sent). He went his way therefore, and washed, and came seeing.

The neighbours therefore, and they which before had seen him that he was blind, said, Is not this he that sat and begged? Some said, This is he: others said, He is like him: but he said, I am he. Therefore said they unto him, How were thine eyes opened? He answered and said, A man that is called Jesus made clay, and anointed mine eyes, and said unto me, Go to the pool of Siloam, and wash: and I went and washed, and I received sight.

Casey Martin

*Young pro golfer Casey Martin changed the look of pro-
fessional golf in 1998 when he won a court ruling allowing
him to use a golf cart during Professional Golfers' Association (PGA) Tour tournaments as an accommodation to
his physical disability. He made a good showing in his first
U.S. Open in June 1998 and won the Lakeland Classic.
Casey plans to play on the Nike Tour again in 1999.*

"In college, a friend of mine brought this story to my attention," said Casey. "She thought it applied to my life. The first time I read it, it kind of hit me like it was my own. It was an answer to a lot of questions about my leg—why God had allowed me to be born a little different."

As a young boy being raised in a Christian home, Casey often prayed for healing for his bad leg. He'd been born with Klippel-Trenaunay-Weber Syndrome, which resulted in vascular problems in one leg. Those problems have left his leg fragile and inefficient at pumping blood back to the heart. This condition is also quite painful. But no matter how hard he prayed, his leg was not healed.

Growing up, Casey also had to deal with people who

apparently felt that prayer was a way of controlling God. That if he just had enough faith and prayed hard enough, God would have to do whatever he (Casey) wanted. "There have been times in my life where people said, 'If you have faith, you'll be healed' or 'You've got to pray for healing.' "

Casey says he's watched people, even on television, "make it seem like if you just have enough faith, you'll be healed. I think there is a lot of that in Christianity today, and it kind of is that if your faith is strong enough, you can be healed. I think God definitely rewards faith, but sometimes it's probably not His will for someone to be healed. Like in my case. I believe it wasn't His will for my leg to be cured, so my prayers for that weren't answered. Does that mean I didn't have faith? I don't think so."

Yet the questions about *why* he had to deal with his physical disability had nagged at him his whole life. He could not help wondering, "Why is this happening to me? Why have I been born different?" When his friend showed him this story, some things suddenly started making sense to him.

"I can't say that I ever got those questions answered in a voice from heaven or anything," Casey states. "But this verse opened my eyes to the fact that God had allowed me to be born with a disability, not because I sinned or because my parents sinned at some point, but that I was created this way for a reason and God was going to be glorified through my leg. At this point, I was playing golf and doing well, but I didn't know how God would be glorified. I always figured He probably would be glorified through my leg and through golf, but at this point some four or five years ago, I had no clue how or when."

Back then, Casey was playing golf at Stanford University and using a cart as an accommodation for his disability. "It really wasn't that big a deal," he remembers. "I used it when I needed it, and it was never a problem. However, I knew that when I turned pro, I wasn't going to be allowed to ride. I'd never seen it on the PGA Tour, so I figured I couldn't do it.

"When I started playing professional golf, I was playing on the mini tours for a couple of years, and steadily my leg got worse. I was really struggling. I couldn't finish out a whole year walking because of the pain I was experiencing. It got to the point, after about two years, where I wasn't having that much success and my leg was really bad, so I had to make a choice. I needed to either get help to play golf—like a cart—or to do something else professionally. I was just praying a lot and trying to find out what I should do."

While Casey was struggling with that decision, a childhood friend who had become an attorney in Eugene, Oregon, began encouraging him to seek an accommodation from the PGA that would allow him to use a cart when he played. This friend kept reminding Casey that a cart was merely an accommodation under the Americans with Disabilities Act.

"I kind of blew it off for a year and thought, 'It's not going to work,'" Casey recalls. "But I started listening more, and it finally came to the point where I was going to wait to see if I made it to the final stages of the Tour qualifying. I would be on the Nike or PGA Tour, and I figured that if I made it to that point, I would pursue a cart, and I did."

Admitting that he was still reluctant to start, Casey

says, "It's been more people telling me I should do it and more people stepping up and saying, 'I want to help you. Will you let me help you get this?' I never felt this was a crusade on my part. It's been more that people were encouraging me to do it.

"As I look back, I think that's maybe how God's done it. I think He's showing Himself strong in that way. He's planting the seeds in people and getting everything together for me as far as lawyers and as far as the whole scenario working together. I could see his hand helping me out instead of me frantically trying to save my career."

Even with the help of friends, getting his cart was not easy. The PGA Tour has fought and continues to fight him every step of the way. He also has had to put up with derogatory comments from people who apparently think the act of walking the golf course is what makes a golfer, not how that golfer hits the ball. Others have taunted him with illogical statements like "Well, they don't allow motor scooters for linebackers in football," as if he hit the ball with the cart.

"That can be frustrating at times," Casey admits. "But I have an understanding of both sides of the issue. However, I have to admit there were definitely times when I got frustrated with the PGA Tour and the commissioner and the whole process. I'd be lying if I said I didn't. I just try to temper it, knowing that there are two sides of the story."

From Casey's point of view, allowing him to use a cart to play is a "no brainer." "I've got a disability in my leg which makes walking difficult and painful. Accommodation in golf is getting a golf cart. They allow golf carts all the time, it doesn't seem like a big deal. It doesn't change the nature of the game. But as golf tends to do, they (the PGA) tried to exempt themselves, saying, 'Hey, that doesn't apply to us. We're exempt from the ADA.' That's how they fought it, but they didn't win. That's how they're still fighting it in the ninth Circuit Court of Appeals."

His faith has been a tremendous help to Casey through the lawsuits and conflict with the PGA. He recalls that the Bible instructs people to love their enemies and says, "These people are not enemies in the sense that some people are enemies. However, they definitely were standing against what I was trying to do, and I guess in some realm, they were considered my enemy. So I definitely tried to love them, and I still try to. It's a challenge at times. I guess that God's given me a peace about it, that it doesn't matter what people think or what people stand in my way. If it's God's will for me to play golf this way, then it's going to happen and I can't be stopped. If I'm stopped, then it's not God's will. If I end up losing the whole cart issue legally, then I'm at peace with that."

So how does Casey see God being glorified through his experiences? He says, "This year (1998), when it became such big news, I had such an opportunity to share, to be seen, to see how God has worked in my life through my leg."

In addition, while Casey has been in the news, he has used his newfound prominence to show people how God has provided for him and been faithful to him in enabling him to pursue his dreams. He states, "God was going to be glorified and display His power through my condition, and I think He's done that in the last year. I trust him completely to do that."

Overcoming Temptation

James 1:12
KING JAMES VERSION

Blessed is the man that endureth temptation: for when he is tried, he shall receive the crown of life, which the Lord hath promised to them that love him.

(NIV VERSION)
(Michael Singletary's Preferred Version)

Blessed is the man who perseveres under trial, because when he has stood the test, he will receive the crown of life that God has promised to those who love him.

Michael Singletary

❦

Being inducted into the Football Hall of Fame was the cap on Michael's athletic career. This former Chicago Bears linebacker and Super Bowl champion was also recognized for his remarkable skills by being named NFL Most Valuable Player (MVP) twice and playing in ten Pro Bowl games. Today, Michael is a motivational speaker, consultant, and author. His latest book is Daddy's Home at Last.

A man of deep faith, Michael has many Bible stories that he considers his favorites. Being asked to name only one gave him pause, then he responded, "Since James is my all-time favorite, I guess I'd better go with that verse."

Michael's verse first came to his attention in the mid-1980s. He recalls, "I think at that particular time, I was going through some things in my life. I had a lot of dreams and goals that I had set, and I guess what happened is that I had achieved those goals and it was a struggle doing it. At the same time, I was in the middle of a transition in my life. From the outside looking in, many people would have thought, 'Wow! this guy has the world by the tail!' I had accomplished a lot—had just gone to the Super

Bowl, had just gotten married, was making good money. I was defensive MVP that year and everything was great, but on the inside, I was very frustrated, very angry, and lonely. Every goal that I had set out to do, I had achieved. I still was not fulfilled.

"It was at that time that I chose to take a snapshot of my life and look at it," Michael states. "Where am I going? What have I done? If I continue in the state I am in, where will I end up?

"I sat down and began to ponder that. I realized that I didn't have an anchor in my life. I didn't have any truth in my life. Everything was conditional. If I do this, then I'll do that. If I can accomplish this, then maybe I'll feel good. But nothing was an anchor, so I was in search for the truth."

Michael adds, "I made up my mind that year to read the entire Bible. The goal was that I would know exactly what the Bible said and what it meant for me. I had talked about the Bible. I had prayed and everything else. But I'd never read the Bible."

Not having read the Bible is not uncommon in our society, but Michael was the son of a Pentecostal minister, so he was exposed to religion in a big way as a child. He describes his adult attitude toward God as "religious and not spiritual." He knew a lot of Bible stories, had heard a lot of theology, but had not made the personal leap from knowing facts in his head to knowing God in his heart.

As he was reviewing his life "snapshot," Michael felt that the Lord was with him, helping him to review his life and determine what he could do to achieve the anchoring he knew he needed.

"I needed to see myself for what I was," Michael remembers. "That was very difficult. I was a hypocrite because I was saying at the time that I was a Christian and I really wasn't, because at that particular time in my life, I was very deceitful. I'd say one thing and do another. Depending on which group of people I was around was how I acted, so that made me a hypocrite. If I was in church, I'd say, Hallelujah!, Praise God!, whatever. When I was at a party, I'd do something else."

When reminded that he is judging himself harshly, Michael responds, "It's an honest look, and that's why it was so very difficult to look at myself. But I'm a firm believer that until you come to grips with where you are in life, you really can't go forward.

"So I was sort of stuck in a rut. My wheels were turning, going nowhere, and for the first time in my life, I saw myself for what I was, and I didn't like that. I remember saying to myself, 'Lord, I'm here and I don't want to be here. I want to know who I am and I want to have firm convictions. I want to go forward with my life, but right now I can't.' "

Realizing that he could not change his life by himself, Michael prayed an earnest prayer that God would help him become a "new creation," a completely new man who would be all the strong and virtuous things he knew he wanted to be. "The Lord met me where I was," Michael says simply of that day. "I remember getting up off my knees and realizing that something very wonderful had just happened."

However, real life is often very different from a football game. A game is decided in a matter of hours. Changing a life is a commitment that takes a great deal of time.

"I began at that moment to read my Bible, and I read

it in the morning and in the evening. I read it before I went to bed. I read it while I was in bed. I read my Bible all night, all day, for several weeks, until I finished it. When I finished, I realized that there were some truths that I'd found that I needed to take care of.

"First, I needed to go back and forgive my father, because I hated him for leaving my mother (when Michael was only twelve years old). I hated him for the kind of father he was. The Lord showed me that I could not do that (forgive) without His power, and that was a real struggle. Then I remembered this verse, 'Blessed is the man who perseveres.'

"There were several times when I said to myself, 'You know what? This is crazy! I don't want to call my dad. I don't want to do this. This is too hard. This doesn't even make sense!' I wanted to rationalize, but it was too late, and I had come to a point in my life where I was either going to take the wide road or the narrow road. I had to go forward because of the decision I'd made, so I picked up the phone and called my dad."

Michael and his father had not talked in quite some time, but this was not to be the feel-good reunion of a fairy tale. "We screamed and yelled and everything else," Michael admits. "But when I hung up the phone, I knew that I'd been released for the first time in my life. There was a part of me that was totally in the dark for years, and for the first time, I was released from the curse of unforgiveness. At the time I thought, 'Why is it so important that I go back and forgive my father? I mean, forget him! I'm just going to get on with life.' The Lord showed me that it really wasn't for my father. It was for me. I was the one in bondage. I was the one who was never going to be able to understand what unconditional love was with my wife or my kids.

"There was no doubt in my mind that if I had not taken that step, I would be either divorced or a husband who abused his wife and kids. It was not only life-changing for my generation, I know now that my kids will be blessed. I know that their kids will be blessed to the third and fourth generations, and they will be blessed because of the obedience of one."

As difficult and challenging as it was to forgive his father, Michael knew that he had an even tougher problem to handle before he could say that he'd gotten his life on track.

"The next step was to go to my wife and ask for her forgiveness for our dating years and the time we were engaged when I was unfaithful to her. That was THE most difficult thing that I've ever done in my life," Michael says emphatically.

Asked if she had been aware of his infidelity, Michael responds softly, "No. She knew that there was something, but not that. It took me several weeks to tell her—everything—and that was very difficult. But once again I held on to that verse. I got everything out, everything that was in the closet. I got it out. This is who I am. This is what you married. I'm sorry, and whatever the consequences are, whatever your decision is, we'll live with that."

Understandably, his wife needed some time to deal with the emotional trauma of realizing that he had betrayed her. It took time, too, to rebuild the trust she had believed they shared. For about a year and a half, Michael struggled with the aftermath of his confession. "Through that whole time," he remembers, "I felt that I was in a dark tunnel and the Lord was holding my hand. He was the light—the only light. I felt that this verse was the one he used to bless me. There were times I wanted to let go and say, 'You know what? Forget it! This doesn't make sense. It's too hard.' But I persevered. Blessed is the man who perseveres under trial, for when he has stood the test, THEN he will see the crown."

Like many people who have fought hard to straighten out their life and build a strong relationship with God, Michael values the "crown of life" that the Bible promises to those who persevere. "The crown of life that I have now is the crown that cannot be taken," he states firmly. "It's the crown that man can't put a value on. It's a crown that I don't deserve. It's a crown that I'm wearing because He's (Jesus) wearing a crown, and what this crown means to me is everything."

In addition to—or perhaps because of—the commitment that Michael has made to persevere, as his Bible verse instructs, he now has the anchor, his faith, and the life that he was desperately searching for back when he first contemplated the "snapshot" he had taken of his life.

He and his wife, Kim, have built a loving home for their seven children, and he is able to provide the kind of fatherly guidance for them that he so profoundly missed as a child. He is able to do work he loves and return blessings to his community through his volunteer commitments, including serving on the board of Pro Athletes Outreach and participating in NFL-sponsored charity events. Best of all, he can honestly say something that everyone wishes for themselves, "I love what I do. I have a lot of time to spend with my family. I'm having the time of my life!"

Romans 8:28

We know that all things work together for good to them that love God, to them who are the called according to his purpose.

Pat Day

꧁꧂

*Hall of Fame jockey Pat Day has over seventy-three hun-
dred wins in more than thirty-four thousand horse races.
The rider with the third most wins of all time, behind Wil-
lie Shoemaker and Laffit Pincay, Jr., Day continues to
thrill racing enthusiasts across the country.*

As a successful young jockey, Bible verses were about
the farthest thing from Pat Day's mind. "My mother
and father did an outstanding job laying a firm foundation. Raised me in a Christian home. It's not their fault I
waited," says Pat of his commitment to God. Until early
1984, he was known as a man who worked hard and
partied hard.

All that changed suddenly when he decided to commit
his life to Christ in January 1984. The change in his life
was instant and permanent. Gone were the heavy drinking
and drugs; in their place were a positive attitude and activities. Pat admits that his wife, Sheila, was initially puz-
zled by this change in him. She'd always been supportive,
but now it was like she was married to a completely different man. It took over a year, but she realized that his

commitment was the real thing and has joined him in his faith.

However, even committing his life to Christ did not change everything about him. Pat still loved to win. He still hated to lose. He still somehow felt the results were all up to him.

In one dramatic moment, he learned the truth. The 1984 Breeders' Cup in Hollywood Park, California, was a highly charged race. Along with the normal tensions that accompany a high-profile race, there had been some bumping and jostling on the track. Even though Pat felt that he and his mount, Wild Again, had won, there was a nerve-racking ten-minute wait after the race before the horse following him was disqualified for causing the problem, and Pat mounted Wild Again to go to the Winner's Circle.

He remembers that remarkable moment. "We were walking around in the circle, waiting for all the people to get lined up and get ready for the pictures. As we turned to face the grandstand, all the people were clapping and screaming. It was a very joyous occasion. I gotta be honest with you, at that point in time, God was the farthest thing from my mind. I was pretty pumped and pretty high on myself. I thought I'd be a little bit of a showman there. I'd take my helmet off and wave it at the crowd.

"As my hand touched my helmet, the audible voice of God said, 'It wasn't them, it was me.' And I understood and recognized at that moment that it was God who had orchestrated that—allowed me to be a part of that—and had brought the victory to pass. I went ahead and took my helmet off, but I no longer acknowledged the crowd.

I looked to heaven and just said, 'Thank you Jesus.' It was a very emotional moment for me."

Yes, winning was great, and now Pat had a clear idea of the support he was receiving that enabled him to win. But he still didn't win every race. He kept wondering why not. What was the difference?

About this time, while he was reading the Bible, a verse jumped out at him. It was Romans 8:28: "We know that all things work together for good to them that love God, to them who are the called according to his purpose." This verse helped him understand that whatever happened, God could use it and him for good.

"I laid hold of that," Pat states firmly. "Not that I gave up on the winning and losing, but I just trusted that God was in the middle of all that I've done and that He was, in fact, working this out for my good and His glory, as long as I would allow Him to work in and through me by the power of His Holy Spirit. My fervent prayer today is that I will be either a humble winner or a gracious loser."

Pat has been challenged to live up to that prayer on many occasions. One of the more dramatic times when the prayer and the verse came together was in the 1996 Preakness Stakes. Pat remembers, "I was riding a horse called Prince of Thieves. I had ridden the horse in the Lexington Stakes. I rode him back in the Kentucky Derby and he ran third. Shortly after that, Grindstone, the winner of that race, was injured and retired. Jerry Bailey was the rider of that horse and was in peak form. The trainer of Prince of Thieves, Mr. Lucas, opted to go with Jerry for the Preakness as opposed to letting me ride the horse. Obviously, I was a little bit hurt. I felt that I had ridden the horse as well as it could be ridden in the Derby, and I thought he had a pretty good chance in the Preakness. But as I said, Mr. Lucas opted to take me off.

"I secured a mount on a horse called Louis Quatorze. It had run in the Derby, but it had run very bad. Horrible performance. Anyhow, we secured a mount on him for the Preakness. He was a bit of a long shot. As it turned out, Louis Quatorze went right to the lead, made all the pace, and won in very handy fashion.

"When that happened, it just confirmed to me that laying hold of Romans 8:28 gives me great confidence. I go out there and do the very best I can, and if I win, praise God. If I lose, praise God. Because I know that God's going to work it out for my good and His glory as long as I allow Him to work in and through me."

Pat cautions people to remember to take the whole verse to heart, not just the first part. He has personally experienced that "all things work together for good to them that love God." At the same time, he states firmly that it would not have happened if he was not one of the people who "are the called according to his (God's) purpose."

"I constantly pray, 'God, I want to be in Your will. I want to do what You'd have me to do. I want to be the person You'd have me to be,' and in so doing, I have the confidence of knowing I'm where He would have me be and doing what He would have me do. Obviously, if I would just leave God out of the equation, if I would fail to seek His will and His design for my life, I couldn't very well take hold of the first part of that promise. That's like people who drink all their life and now they're dying because their kidneys are failing or their liver is shot and they want to lay hold of that promise. Well, God's will for your life did not include drinking to the degree that you ruined your health. In that respect, you reap what you sow. You have to suffer the consequences of your actions. It wouldn't be fair to be outside the will of God and expect that all things will work to your good."

In most areas of life, the problems are not resolved as quickly as in a horse race. People who are trying to lead a godly life can find themselves going through long periods where nothing seems to be right—and nothing seems to be "working together for good" for them. Pat counsels, "Obviously, when you're in the middle of the storm, it's hard to see with the storm swirling all around you. You can't see behind you or in front of you. But once you get through the storm and have gone past, then you can see so clearly and will be able to see why those things had to happen in that manner in order for you to be where you are and be the person that you are. What I would say to somebody in that situation is certainly don't turn loose of God's hand. Hang on to your faith."

When Pat faces tough times or tough questions, he holds on to his faith—and looks down to his wrist. There, where he can easily see it, is a gift that his daughter, Irene, gave him. It is a bracelet that is popular with young people across the country. The simple message printed on it is "WWJD," What Would Jesus Do? "This bracelet is a reminder to me," Pat acknowledges. "Especially in difficult situations.

"I understand and recognize that God won't keep me in this situation always. My career as a jockey will one day be over, and God has other things for me to do," Pat says thoughtfully. Whatever the future holds, he will continue to believe and live Romans 8:28, and believe that while some days will be happy and others will hold sadness, all things in his life will work to his good, because he loves God and seeks to live according to God's plan.

Afterword

I hope you have enjoyed reading about these very special people and how favorite Bible verses or stories have become very important in their lives.

If you have a Bible story or verse that is special to you, I'd love to hear from you. You can E-mail me at donna@albrechts.com, visit my web site at www.albrechts.com/donna, or write to me at P.O. Box 21423, Concord, CA 94521.

If I'm able to share your story in an upcoming book, I will get in touch with you for permission and to set up an interview.

—Donna G. Albrecht